TIE A
YELLOW RIBBON

First published April 2006
Copyright © Tim Manns and David Bull, 2006

Published by HAGIOLOGY PUBLISHING
170 Westbury Road
Bristol BS9 3AH

ISBN 0-9534474-6-4

Designed by Elizabeth Porter, www.porterlizz-graphic-design.co.uk, Bristol
Printed and bound in Great Britain by The Bath Press

TIE A YELLOW RIBBON

How The Saints Won The Cup

TIM MANNS

with additional material, and overall editing, by David Bull

in association with

and

SOUTHERN
Daily Echo

Dedications

Tim Manns

This book is dedicated to the memory of my Mum, Mollie, who passed away on
15 December 2005, and to my Dad, Harry, who is a lifelong Saints fan.
I also thank my lovely wife, Anna, for her patience and understanding.

David Bull

For Fred Goddard and George Titt, two uncles forever associated with
my being a Saints fan, who have died since I stopped by in Salisbury,
to deliver our previous Hagiology book to them.

In celebrating the FA Cup run of 30 years ago, we remember those we have lost since the climax of that run at Wembley.

PETER OSGOOD and BOBBY STOKES.
always room-mates and, here, Wembley bath-mates.

The coaches JIM CLUNIE, GEORGE HORSFALL and JOHN McGRATH;
and the man who spied, and reported, on all six opponents, TED BATES.

The front cover shows a few of those players who have just won the Cup.

Back row (*left to right*) Channon, Turner, McCalliog, Gilchrist (behind the ribbon); Bennett (peeping under the Cup); Blyth (ducking forward); Don Taylor (in red); Rodrigues. Front: Osgood, Steele.

The back cover illustration is a *Southern Daily Echo* photo of the open-top bus arriving at the Civic Centre on Sunday 2 May 1976.

The 12 signed coloured photos at the top of pages 114-138 are from Ray Mursell's collection. We believe these to be the copyright of the *Southern Daily Echo*, which has been a major source of illustrations throughout the book. The other photos known, or thought, to be from the *Echo* appear at pages 4,5,7,11,12(top), 16 (both), 23 (top), 29, 30 (both), 34, 36, 39, 42, 47, 50, 51, 52 (bottom), 60 (left), 63, 65 (both), 66, 70, 71 (top), 74, 78, 79, 88, 94, 103 (bottom), 105 (bottom), 107 (top), 108, 109, 112 (bottom), 115 (bottom), 128, 139, 142.

Other photos of known copyright are from the following professional sources:

Southampton FC (*saintsfcpics.com*): pages 84, 86 (bottom), 91 (bottom), 106, 116 (top), 130, 133 (bottom), 137.
Birmingham Mail: 10, 12 (bottom), 22, 23 (bottom).
Empics: (v), (ix), 85, 87.
Hy Money: 49, 52 (top), 70, 89 (both), 98 (both), 102, 123 (top).
Roger Elliott, Salisbury Newspapers: 121.
Selsdon Park Hotel: 123 (bottom).
Bill Selwyn: 129 (bottom).

Further illustrations have come from the private collections of Billy Anderson, 18; John Ashton, 37, 40; Mary Bates, 110 (bottom left); Pete Brook, 135; Elaine Bushrod, 71 (bottom); Michael Channon Jr, 129 (top); Richard Ember, 125; Paul Gilchrist, 127; Ian Gordon, 110 (bottom right); Nigel Hale, 72, 76 (all); Peter Hurn, 53; Andy Kershaw, 67, 103 (top), 110 (top); Tony Matthews 25, 31; Steve Mullins, 151; Ray Mursell, 132; Chris Newman, 95 (bottom); Lynn Osgood 133 (top); David Peach, 119; Phil Rawlings, 80; Herbie Taylor, 77; Ray Terris, 60 (right); George Tomkins, 54 (both), 81, 83; Ian Turner, 116 (bottom); John Warren, 100 (bottom two); Dave Webster, 100 (top two); Glen Williams, 95 (top); Peggy Worlock, 110 (middle).

The remaining images are mostly from Duncan Holley's collection, but a few have come, along with most of the programmes used, from Gary Chalk.

Editor's note: The photo of a Welsh trio on page 115 was taken by a fan at the *Dell Diamond* launch and kindly presented to me. I acknowledge the gift and am pleased to have been able to use it here, but regret that I have no recall of who that fan was. Apologies.

Contents

Road to Wembley — 1

The Boys of '76 — 113

Foreword

by Tommy Docherty

"I wanted to shoot myself"

I probably didn't make many friends in Southampton after the draw was made for the semi-final of the 1976 FA Cup because I said that the real Cup Final would be played at Hillsborough between us and Derby. They were a great side that year and were going for the double. So, after we won that game, I couldn't see Southampton beating us.

I would have mortgaged the house on us winning the Final, but you only play as well as you are allowed. On reflection, we probably reached our peak before the Final and, on the day, Southampton were the better side. I had a terrific team but none of them performed to the best of their ability at Wembley and Southampton deservedly won it.

It was very disappointing but, if I had to lose to anyone, it would have been Southampton Football Club and I was delighted for them.

After the final whistle, I wanted to shoot myself but there were players on the other side that I had real affection for and wanted to congratulate. Among them were Jimmy McCalliog, who I had managed, and Ossie, one of the greatest players I have ever seen and managed. Lawrie McMenemy and his coaches were such nice people and I felt a part of me was in the Southampton dressing-room. Then there was Mick Channon, who was such a great lad and whose timing was so wonderful with his testimonial coming 48 hours after the Final. And, of course, little Bobby Stokes who scored the winning goal, God rest his soul.

A few hours after the Final, I phoned Lawrie to reiterate my congratulations. I was very disappointed for my team but I was delighted for everyone at Southampton. Lawrie said he hoped we would go back and win it the next season and of course we did, but not before drawing Saints in the Fifth Round.

My affection for Southampton goes way back to when I played for Preston and we would come to The Dell. I got to know Ted Bates quite well and always admired him, not only as a manager but as a person. He was a lovely man, as was George Reader the Chairman. They were always very hospitable when you went there. Win, lose or draw they were always the same. They were lovely people.

This is why it is my pleasure and privilege to write the foreword to this book, which I am sure will bring back many happy memories of a very special team and football club.

Preface

by David Bull

I hope I never tire of being impressed – excited, even – by somebody coming up with a clever idea I'd never have thought of.

That's what happened when Tim Manns suggested a 30th anniversary book on the Saints' 1976 Cup run. I'd got used to thinking of books on Saints' history in terms of long definable periods, the shortest span in half-a-dozen Hagiology publications to date being 57 seasons. So a book on eight games, played over four months, was novel.

But Tim was calling his idea "Boys of '76" and, as I knew of two books on England's World Cup win that were titled or sub-titled "Boys of '66", I had a sense of how such a limited focus could be developed, *without* any padding or spin, into a hardback book.

The proposal, to which we've adhered, was for a two-parter. The first relives the eight games through the eyes of those who played in them – and those of a few other participants acknowledged by Tim below. In the second, those players tell readers what they've done since. Such where-are-they-now stories are an ever-popular feature of football magazines and match-day programmes, but they are jolly hard work: while blurred memories of what has happened in Saints' games can be readily checked, for accuracy, in the various records published by Gary Chalk and Duncan Holley, ascertaining what really happened, in the late 1970s and early 1980s, at clubs from Crystal Palace to Cape Town City proved a considerably tougher proposition.

I was assisted in that task by Gary Chalk, the book's statistician (see especially pages 145-148) and archivist. He occasionally drew, in turn, on the extensive knowledge of Leigh Edwards, but I still needed to consult an unprecedented number of club historians and collectors, as acknowledged on page (xiv).

And how about the fans? We agreed to invite memories and memorabilia, which I took responsibility for collating as complements to Tim's player-based accounts. We are grateful to all of the contributing fans, including those who sent us material that we did not use – for various reasons that we have tried privately to explain. Involving the fans had two impacts on the presentation of this book. First, it helped – along with the checking of players' memories – to give me a full-time role, so Tim suggested my name accompany his on the cover. Secondly, it now seemed inappropriate to have a title that focused on the players alone. *Tie a Yellow Ribbon* conveys, we hope, how we *all* celebrated – players and fans alike.

The photos received from fans bring a splash of colour to the latter half of the book, beginning with the Final. We had only two coloured images from the previous rounds but decided to print them, in common with the programme covers for those games, in black-and-white. This divide not only made financial sense but also seemed symbolically appropriate. If some of the coloured photos from the fans are less sharp than you might expect from your camera today, they surely capture what the weekend of 1-2 May 1976 was like – not only for those who took them, and have preserved them, but for thousands of others who were part of that cavalcade of colour. And how well they inter-mingle – don't you think? – with the professionals' black-and-white images that characterised football photography of that era.

For the majority of those images, we have relied, as ever, on the *Southern Daily Echo* (to which we have referred, in the text, as the *Echo*, whether our source was the *Football Echo* or a weekday edition). We are grateful to Stewart Dunn and Ian Murray for permission to reproduce those *Echo* photos and to Jez Gale for all of his help in retrieving them. The *Birmingham Mail* kindly allowed us to use images from Saints' two visits to the West Midlands, while several photos of the semi-final and/or Final have been supplied by Empics (where Laura Hitchcock was so helpful) and by Hy Money, who was so generous, patient and enthusiastic in satisfying our searches. The club, itself, not only allowed us to reproduce its limited holding of photos from 1976, but has contributed some recent photos, including a few commissioned by us.

This, and other professional, help with photos is acknowledged in the credits on page (vi), where we have identified also the private collectors to whom we are indebted. A special thanks to Ray Mursell, for the signed coloured photographs. Otherwise, Duncan Holley, as ever, led the way, often assisted by Gary Chalk. Most of the photos thus obtained are probably *Echo* copyright and, even in some cases where we are not certain, are credited as such. The risk, when obtaining illustrations in this second-hand fashion, is that we fail to acknowledge the relevant copyright, let alone pay for reproduction rights. We trust that any copyright-holders, whose rights we may thus have infringed, will contact us.

We had access to some invaluable scrapbooks, which not only helped us to check stories but also to point us to photos that we needed to obtain and use. Unfortunately, some of the originals of that era – whether from a national, or local, newspaper – are no longer retrievable. Thus, we were unable to acquire a glorious *Daily Express* photo of Mick Channon, but had to make do with the cutting at page 107. And while the *Echo* has a splendid library of photos from the semi-final draw onwards, few photos of the early rounds were available in their original form. But since we felt we had to produce some photographic evidence of the goals scored in those games, you will see that we have done so either by printing some grainy images or by reducing the size, so that the inferior quality is less glaring.

The taking, storage and retrieval of football photographs has changed considerably of late, so historians of the club's recent endeavours will not have these problems. As it is, we have done our best with what we have been able to trace and we thank those newspapers, agencies and individuals who have done their best to help us illustrate the Cup run of 1976.

The task of integrating the selected photos with the text was undertaken for us by Liz Porter, who cheerfully and diligently did justice – I hope you agree – to the material we had obtained from fans, various back-stage participants and the Boys of '76.

Introduction

by Tim Manns

At the start of the 1975-76 season I followed my normal routine which was to go to the first home game with my three mates, Steve Gilbert, Steve Eyers and Brian Longland.

As we were waiting for the game against West Brom to start, we looked at the programme and, in particular, studied the fixture list. Brian looked up and said, "I see this season's Cup Final is on 1 May. That's the day I'm getting married. I bet this will be the year Saints get to Wembley."

Oh, how we laughed.

The four of us left The Dell, as injury time approached at the end of our Third Round match against Aston Villa. The Saints were losing 1-0 and we couldn't see any way that Brian's big day would be spoiled. Then we heard the unmistakable sound of a goal being celebrated as we walked along Milton Road. It was the last time I ever left a match before the final whistle.

As the Cup run progressed, and after each successive win, Brian looked progressively more concerned. For reasons that escape me now, the four of us didn't go to the semi-final together, but we met outside Stamford Bridge afterwards. Among the huge throng of smiling, cheering faces, Brian was – to use a tabloid expression – ashen-faced.

He wasn't laughing now.

To my knowledge, there were only three men at Brian's wedding: the groom, his dad and the bride's dad. We haven't seen each other for a few years now, but the last time I reminded him of 1 May 1976, a wistful look passed across his face and I realised he would never quite get over missing the Cup Final.

At the time, I was working in Poole. All thoughts of a career in broadcasting lay in the future, for now I was an assistant quantity surveyor on the Poole Arts Centre project. All my colleagues knew I was a Saints fan and on the Friday my boss, Peter Evans, asked me for a prediction of the score. I told him I didn't want to put a jinx on things by saying what I thought would happen, so I wrote my prediction on a piece of paper, folded and stapled it and told him to open it at 5.00 pm the next day.

Even now, I can hardly believe I put "Saints 1, Man Utd 0 (Stokes)". In fact, the only part I got wrong was that I thought the goal would come in the first half. On the way to London the next day, I worked out, from the morning papers, that a double bet of a couple of pounds on the result and the first scorer would win me enough money to buy a car, if I was right. Unfortunately, our coach took us straight to the Wembley car park and it proved impossible to place that bet.

When the goal went in, I remember feeling as though I might explode with excitement and then, as the clock counted down, I was actually relieved I didn't have money riding on the result. It was tense enough, anyway, but the thought of a large (in my impoverished terms) win being in the balance would have been too much to bear.

With that Cup run's 30th anniversary looming, I found myself working for Southampton FC. Through my job at THE SAINT, I had become friends with Peter Rodrigues, Peter Osgood and Hugh Fisher and they all promised their support if I decided to undertake the writing of this book. Next, I asked David Bull whether the Hagiology team were planning anything along these lines. I would have stepped aside if they were already on the case, but they had no such plans and, to my delight, offered to support me in such an endeavour.

I approached Andrew Cowen, Managing Director of the club, who gave me his permission, provided that I worked with the Hagiology Publishing collective. As I wouldn't have attempted it without them, that condition was happily met. I am grateful, then, to Andrew for his blessing and to the Hagiology team for their support and encouragement. They are all totally dedicated to the Saints and their knowledge of the club is unparalleled. They are David Bull, Gary Chalk, Duncan Holley and Dave Juson. In David, I have had the benefit of an editor whose attention to detail is second to none.

And so began a process that has seen me talk to all of the then surviving members of the squad, many of the coaching team and backroom staff and some of the players from the teams we beat along the way. A list of those to whom I am indebted follows overleaf. The name of Lawrie McMenemy is not, however, among them, as he declined to be interviewed. While I respect his decision, it does sadden me that he chose not to contribute to a project that was only ever intended to celebrate his, and his team's, success.

Having suggested we include fans' memories, I was happy for David to assemble them. When I saw the outcome, I was hugely impressed by the way so many people have been able to recall small details of their FA Cup experience. For the life of me, I cannot recall actually buying my ticket, only that I had a precious voucher that enabled me to do so. I do remember that I stood behind the goal with two of my brothers, Phil and Toby, while my dad and my youngest brother, Rob, had seats (Dad's ticket is reproduced on page 72) and it was always very special to me that we were all able to go to the game.

As we came to the end of the writing and editing stage, and just before we went to print, tragedy struck with the death of Peter Osgood. He had been hugely supportive throughout, giving freely of his time to be interviewed, providing contacts for his former team-mates and also offering constant support and encouragement. Although he never got to see the finished work, I hope and trust he would have approved of what we have done.

I make no claim that this is a definitive account of that glorious period in the history of Southampton FC: time has dulled too many memories for that to be possible. I hope that we have managed, however, to capture the essence of what was achieved.

Acknowledgments

Further to expressions, in the previous four pages, of our gratitude for so many kinds of contribution to this book, the acknowledgments below reflect our division of labour in pursuing all those people.

Tim Manns: I am most grateful to Tommy Docherty who kindly agreed to write the foreword and to the following, who all gave generously of their time and allowed me to interview them and without whom this book could not have been written:
Paul Bennett, Mel Blyth, Tony Brown, Mick Channon, Joe Cooke, Steve Coppell, Pat Earles, Bill Ellerington, Hugh Fisher, Paul Gilchrist, Nick Holmes, Keith Honey, Jim McCalliog, Chris Nicholl, Gerry O'Brien, Mike O'Brien, Peter Osgood, David Peach, Peter Rodrigues, Jim Steele, Don Taylor, Peter Taylor, Clive Thomas, Ian Turner, Mickey Walsh and Peggy Worlock.

I would also like to thank several others who helped in many different ways:
Mike Barber, Denis Bundy, Simon Burfield, Robin Caddy, Liz Coley, Will Cope, Jo Dalton, Steve Davies, Stewart Dennis, Ian Dowell, Barry Fox, Jez Gale, Ian Gordon, Graham Hiley, Brian Hunt, Caaren Loten, David Luker, Toby Manns, Tom Manser, Tony Manser, Michael McCartney, Leighton Mitchell, Ian Murray, Tim Orme, Lynn Osgood, Ben Pickles, Phil Shepherd, Chris Smith, Richard Smith, John Warren, Ben Whitmarsh and John Wilson.

David Bull: While Tim was busy doing the interviews and obtaining help from others acknowledged above, my duties were four-fold:

- Pursuing the professional photographers and agencies: individuals have been acknowledged in the preface and/or the photo credits.
- Pestering historians (and various collectors) of other clubs, for some permutation of records, contacts, photos or programmes. I am indebted to John Cross and Gerry Wolstenholme (Blackpool); John Ashton and Dave Pendleton (Bradford City); Paul Christopher (Brockenhurst); Billy Anderson and Peter Raath (Cape Town City); Tom Kelly (Christchurch); Peter Hurn and Ian King (Crystal Palace); Ron Parrott (Hereford United); Ian Nannestad (Lincoln City); Bryan Horsnell (Reading); Richard Walker (Salisbury City); Rob Urwin and Geoff Wilde (Southport); and Tony Matthews (West Bromwich Albion).
- Gaining access to the scrapbooks of Jim Dolbear, John Warren and, most especially, Betty Channon, who also provided tea and mince pies.
- Gathering (with Gary Chalk's help) the memories, photos and other memorabilia of fans whose names appear with their stories and/or in the photo credits.

I am indebted, as ever, to David Barber at the FA library and to the Bristol-based research assistance of Dave Adlem and Mike Swain – plus, on this occasion, Steve Smith. Michael Channon Jr was a constant source of help and I shamelessly exploited Nigel Hale for proof-reading assistance.

Road to Wembley

This section is devoted to the eight games that Southampton played between 3 January and 1 May 1976, to win the FA Cup.

The coverage of each game follows a common format:

♦   The programme cover and line-ups.
♦   The highlights (drawn from newspaper reports and the accounts in *In That Number*).
♦   A match report, derived mainly from the memories of those who played for the Saints in that game.

Each account also includes three or four display boxes

From the other side… the recall of an opponent, exclusively interviewed for this book.

On the march… memories of the fans, just one or two for each round, but with rather more for the semi-final and so many, for the Final, that sub-headings become necessary.

The man in the middle… The grey boxes for the Final also include the recollections of the referee, Clive Thomas.

In other news… A lot has happened since 1976. So as to remind you of what was going on at the time – mainly in the worlds of politics and entertainment – we have selected a few highlights, match by match.

The memories derived from the interviews conducted for this section of the book have occasionally been supplemented by quotations from interviews for previous publications: for details, see page 19 below.

Third Round

The Dell   **3 January 1976**

SOUTHAMPTON 1   ASTON VILLA 1

Fisher   Gray

Att: 24,138   Referee: David Wallace

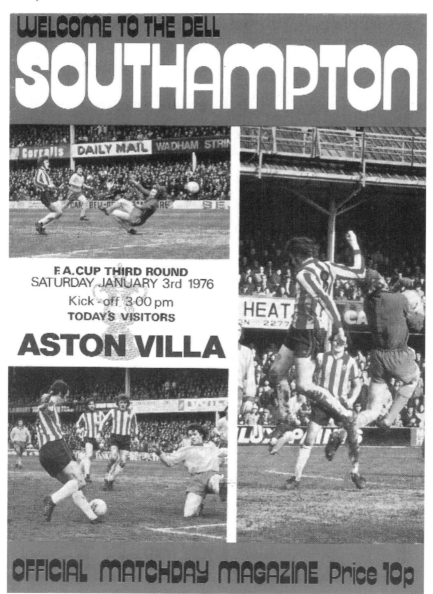

TEAM CHECK

SAINTS		VILLA	
Red & White stripes, Black shorts, White socks	CHANGES	Claret and Blue Shirts and Blue Shorts.	CHANGES
Ian Turner		**1** John Burridge	
Peter Rodrigues		**2** John Gidman	
David Peach		**3** John Robson	
Nick Holmes		**4** Ian Ross	
Mel Blyth		**5** Chris Nicholl	
Jim Steele		**6** Leighton Phillips	
Hugh Fisher		**7** Ray Graydon	
Mike Channon		**8** John Deehan	
Bobby Stokes		**9** Andy Gray	
Jim McCalliog		**10** Ian Hamilton	
Paul Gilchrist		**11** Frank Carrodus	
		12	

Team Changes

SAINTS	12 Earles
VILLA	12 Aitken

Highlights

Villa's first corner nodded on by Nicholl and in by Graydon but disallowed.

21 mins: Nicholl headed against post.

25 mins: Gilchrist booked for foul on Hamilton; nearly sent off for protesting.

30 mins: McCalliog played one-two with Channon and shot just wide.

44 mins: Gilchrist volleyed Fisher's cross just wide.

HT 0-0

Holmes needed treatment after being kicked in stomach by Deehan.

62 mins: Channon shot from left wing, Burridge dived full length to save.

64 mins: 0-1 Nicholl hit bar, but **Gray** tapped in rebound.

79 mins: Gilchrist replaced by Earles (making his debut).

89 mins: 1-1 Peach cross touched by Earles to Channon, back to **Fisher**, who shot home through crowded area.

FT 1-1

On the first Saturday of January 1975, Saints had lost at home in the Third Round of the FA Cup to First Division West Ham who had gone on to win the Cup. At approaching twenty-to-five on the corresponding Saturday a year later, once again at The Dell, First Division Aston Villa led by the only goal of the game. Andy Gray had scored midway through the second half and anyone brave enough to predict that either of these two sides might go on and lift the trophy would surely have plumped for Ron Saunders's Villa. They had won the League Cup the previous season, as well as promotion, and closing this game out should have been well within their capabilities.

Hugh Fisher's last-minute equaliser changed all that and set in motion a train of events that lifted the spirits of a city as well as being the catalyst for a glorious era in the history of a football club that had, hitherto, seemed never to believe in itself enough to achieve lasting glory.

For Mike Channon, who would play in 40 FA Cup-ties for the club, there was definitely a sense of destiny: "It was strange, but things happened in the Cup run which were almost weird. Afterwards, I said, 'Well, Hughie's just scored; we'll win the FA Cup now.' He never scored."

It would be fairer to say that Fisher *almost* never scored. Eleven goals in 356 competitive appearances for the club was, as he is the first to admit, a modest return. Nevertheless, here was a vital goal and one that the Scot, who had joined from Blackpool nine years previously, remembers well.

Watched by Stokes (No. 9) and Channon (No. 8), Gilchrist takes a left-footed shot.

Editor's note: *When Dave Juson came up with this photo for FULL-TIME at THE DELL in 2001, he and I initially agreed it was of a shot by Gilchrist. But there was circumstantial evidence that suggested it was of Fisher scoring his legendary goal. We captioned it as such, only to be ridiculed by Mike Channon for our folly: anyone could see it was Gilchrist. So that's how we described it, in 2003, in IN THAT NUMBER. I hoped we might settle the argument in 2005, by asking Gilchrist if it was he. He wasn't sure but undertook to sit down with Fisher and decide. The outcome? They couldn't decide. But we have: we think it's Gilchrist; and the hoardings, coupled with the policeman on the move, suggest that it's his 44th-minute shot that went wide.*

So the best picture we can offer of Fisher's goal is the grainy effort opposite.

In the last few minutes, it seemed everybody was in the Villa box. I shouldn't have been in there but David Peach crossed, Mick Channon knocked it back into the area and it fell onto my dodgy left peg, the one I usually stand on. I was about 12 yards out and there were lots of players around me. A bit like a golf shot, I just caught it on the sweet spot and I can see it now going low through a ruck of players. I thought it must hit someone but it managed to miss the lot – and John Burridge's hand.

That account omits any mention of another player who was involved in the build-up. Pat Earles had come on, after 79 minutes, as a substitute for Paul Gilchrist, who "had gone into the dressing room so I didn't see the equaliser." Pat stakes his "claim to fame" – in his 11-minute contribution to the Cup run – on laying Peach's cross off to Channon.

The goal would come to mean many things to many people but it was a bit special for the club physiotherapist, Don Taylor. When he took up that post in November 1971, a challenge awaited him: to get Fisher – his "first patient and a long-term one" – back on his feet after breaking his leg, six week's earlier, in a collision with Arsenal's Bob Wilson at The Dell.

Few of Channon's team-mates recall attaching undue significance to Hughie's last-gasp goal, although Mel Blyth claims that "a lot of us thought, with the luck we had to get the equaliser, it might mean a good Cup run." This opening game of what would become the first Cup run he was ever involved in "was the only game that I thought at any stage we were going to lose."

Not that he had a lot of time to think about anything very much as the run developed. Although he had joined the Saints from Crystal Palace 16 months earlier, he had continued living in Sanderstead, south London. He would get up at 5.30 every morning and collect Peter Osgood before driving to The Dell for training. And now he was pre-occupied with the anticipated arrival of his first child in April.

David Peach remembers a struggle, a late equaliser and a draw out of nothing: "we were relieved but we still had to go to Villa Park. The fact that it was Hughie who scored should have been a sign that something different was on." The scorer himself sums up the mood in the home camp after the final whistle.

John Burridge cannot stop the 89th-minute equaliser from Fisher (out of picture).

The dressing room was buzzing afterwards. Obviously it pleased the club because the replay meant money and money was important. As players we were just glad to have another chance.

Across the corridor, Villa manager Ron Saunders was furious, as his centre-half, Chris Nicholl, recalls: "we had been in control and let them back in." He blames his good friend – and future coaching colleague at Southampton – Ray Graydon, for the slip that led to the equaliser.

We thought we were coasting at 1-0 when Ray gave a ball away near the half-way line. I knew we were in trouble from it and the ball came in and was knocked in for the draw. I was really unhappy because we were a First Division side and expected to win.

On the march...

I was just making my way to the back of the Milton Road when we equalised. So, even though I never saw Hughie Fisher's goal, I was in the ground when it was scored.

As I made my way back to the "Football Special" bus, I thought "waste of time us going to Villa Park; we'll never get anything there." I listened to the replay on the radio – or, rather, the score-flashes provided by Radio Solent. So I was wrong about getting anything from Villa Park.

Dave Webster

Being involved in local amateur sport, I missed most of the Cup run. But to this day, I share a joke about this match with a Villa supporter who'd moved down here to work with me at Plessey in Titchfield. With minutes remaining, he was on his way out at the Archers Road end, when he heard a mighty roar, interspersed with some broad Brummie expletives from the terrace above him. So, whenever I ring him, I always announce "Hugh Fisher calling." And, if I write to him, my letter-heading says THE HUGH FISHER APPRECIATION SOCIETY.

David Cheffy

Editor's note: *If eligibility for this Appreciation Society were limited to those who'd stayed around to appreciate Fisher's shot, the membership would be minimal, it seems. And Dave Webster's recollection, both of the goal and of predictions uttered upon leaving the ground, are so similar to those of Tim Manns – as confessed in his introduction – that I am tempted to ask whether* any *Saints fan left The Dell, both having seen the* equaliser *and* remotely hopeful about the replay.

Obviously, I didn't know at the time that I would go to Southampton but these were the two main clubs in my career. I came to The Dell in 1977, as one of the older players, in the way that Lawrie built his sides.

But when I became manager, we had to move the older players out and bring the youngsters through – which brought the wage bill down and then later brought in a lot of money in transfer fees when we sold them. We always did better in the Cup competitions, but following Lawrie meant the fans had raised expectations. It was a difficult job, anyway, but following Lawrie…!

And I remember a dressing room with Peter Shilton in one corner, Joe Jordan in another and Mark Dennis in another.

It seems to me now that any new manager has to learn the job and it is probably unwise to put a novice in charge of a Premiership side. It was a terrific time in my life.

Chris Nicholl

June 1977: "older players" Nicholl (30) and Phil Boyer (28) sign for the Saints, as McMenemy rebuilds for promotion.

In other news...

The Cod War might now seem like a joke, but it was very serious at the time. Iceland claimed to be economically dependent on fishing but the UK fish catch was worth over £20m to our economy. The Icelandic Prime Minister, Hr Hallgrimmson, had already warned of a coming confrontation when, on 7 January, the frigate *HMS Andromeda* collided with the gunboat *Thor*.

Both sides claimed the other had rammed them and the dispute would continue for another six months until NATO negotiated an agreement that limited Britain to using 24 trawlers for an annual catch of 50,000 tonnes.

Cod stocks have continued to decline and there are now, of course, regular calls for a total ban on cod fishing.

In the previous week, Radio 1 had broadcast a Bay City Rollers special and, soon after, DJ Johnnie Walker left for America. He had been highly critical of the station's play-listing such "manufactured" bands.

Number 1 in the charts was Queen's *Bohemian Rhapsody* and the highlight of the week's TV was the return of *The Morecambe and Wise Show* on BBC1.

Third Round Replay

Villa Park   **7 January 1976**

ASTON VILLA 1   SOUTHAMPTON 2

Graydon   McCalliog 2
Att: 44,623   Referee: David Wallace

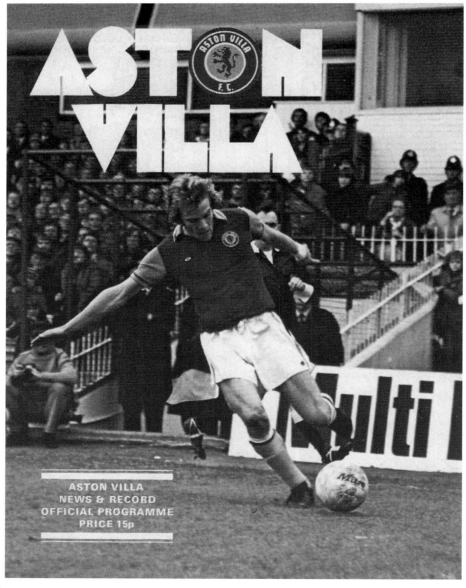

ASTON VILLA Claret and Blue Shirts, White Shorts	TEAM CHANGES	SOUTHAMPTON Red H White Striped Shirts, Black Shorts	TEAM CHANGES
1 JOHN BURRIDGE		1 IAN TURNER	
2 JOHN GIDMAN		2 PETER RODRIGUES	
3 JOHN ROBSON		3 DAVID PEACH	
4 IAN ROSS		4 NICK HOLMES	
5 CHRIS NICHOLL		5 MEL BLYTH	
6 LEIGHTON PHILLIPS		6 JIM STEELE	
7 RAY GRAYDON		7 HUGH FISHER	
8 JOHN DEEHAN		8 MIKE CHANNON	
9 ANDY GRAY		9 BOBBY STOKES	
10 IAN HAMILTON		10 JIM McCALLIOG	
11 FRANK CARRODUS		11 PAUL GILCHRIST	
12		12	

Team Changes

VILLA   12 Aitken

SAINTS   9 Osgood   11 Stokes   12 Gilchrist

Highlights

31 mins: 1-0 Osgood squared pass to Channon, crossed to **McCalliog**, who headed in from 6 yds.

39 mins: 1-1 Peach under-hit back-pass, **Graydon** intercepted and beat Turner.
HT 1-1

66 mins: Graydon substituted with muscle strain.

83 mins: Burridge tipped away Rodrigues fierce drive.
90 mins: 1-1

Osgood replaced by Gilchrist during break.
Turner stopped a point-blank header from Deehan.
Peach headed a Nicholl header off line.
Holmes forced magnificent save from Burridge.

103 mins: 2-1 Peach corner hit home, via a deflection, by **McCalliog**.
FT 2-1

The modern convention of replays being staged at least 10 days after the original game would have seemed ridiculous back in the 1970s. So it was that, four days after the drawn match at The Dell, a crowd of nearly 45,000 gathered at Villa Park on a cold, January night for what most must have assumed would be the inevitable progress of the top-division side into the next round.

The team travelled by train. According to Jim Steele, they went via London and passed within sight of Wembley's twin towers. He was not impressed when Mick Channon took a look across and "said 'We'll be there' and we're all going 'Micky, get real and have another drink.' We thought he was joking."

A home tie against Second Division strugglers, Blackpool, awaited the winners and Saints keeper Ian Turner took some inspiration from the undue confidence of his opposite number.

> John Burridge said how he was looking forward to playing his former club,
> Blackpool, in the next round. I thought he was being a bit cheeky in assuming
> Villa would go through.

Burridge's confidence must have taken a knock when Jim McCalliog opened the scoring. Chris Nicholl remembers "a trick" from Peter Osgood, back in the side after watching Saturday's match from the stand, which led to the goal.

It wasn't all plain sailing for the visitors, though. Villa were soon level, following an error from the normally reliable David Peach. An under-hit back-pass – "I didn't look" – allowed Graydon in for the equaliser. Peach "wasn't particularly popular at half-time but, from then on, we played great and deserved to beat them."

Against one of football's classic backgrounds – Archibald Leitch's magnificent Trinity Road Stand –
the Southampton defence (*left to right:* Turner, Steele, Gilchrist and Blyth) holds firm.
So the grandeur to Villa, but a Fourth-Round tie for the Saints.

Despite the defensive lapse, Saints centre-backs both believed victory was theirs for the taking. Steele remembers that it seemed easy and that they had the game under control. For Mel Blyth, it was a case of being fully prepared and focussed.

> We were up for it that night and we were a better Cup side than a League side. There is no such thing as a perfect night for a match but it was to our liking, so we just went out there and did it.

That Blyth was fit to play was a credit to Don Taylor's efforts to prepare him and get him through the pain of a back injury which, at that point, had not been fully diagnosed.

There were no goals in the second half, so extra-time was needed. Lawrie McMenemy was always at his best when it came to motivating his men and Peach believes he got it just right with his extra-time briefing: "He told us to keep doing what we had been doing, because we deserved to win. We already knew we would be at home in the next round – which helps, too."

Lawrie McMenemy gets it "just right" as he briefs Steele and Rodrigues (No. 2) before extra-time. Blyth (No. 5) confers with trainer Clunie.

Channon, Hugh Fisher and Nick Holmes all share the view that Saints' performance that night was one of their very best. Holmes accepts that they had been outplayed in the first game but "couldn't believe how much we dominated them in the replay, especially a Second Division side against one from the First."

For Channon, that was a false distinction: "we were different class. They may have been a First Division side but we had First Division players. In those days, there wasn't the gulf there is now between the top two divisions."

Although only two days away from his 32nd birthday, Fisher didn't find the 120 minutes too much.

> The pitch was good – and I could always get up and down, because my fitness was always pretty good. We had good support, too, and I do remember the fans giving us good backing.

McCalliog's second goal settled the affair. But, then, Villa Park was a lucky ground for him: "I played there when I made my debut for Sheffield Wednesday, after I joined them from Chelsea – for a British record fee for a teenager – and I scored there in the FA Cup semi-final for them in 1966."

McCalliog's shot is deflected past Chris Nicholl (No. 5) to give the Saints an extra-time lead.

The next morning, the squad was heading north for the scheduled Saturday League fixture at Blackburn. That meant a night out in Birmingham. Never a team to need an excuse to let their hair down, they were "on a high," Fisher recalls: "I can remember Ossie running around with a policeman's helmet on at about two in the morning. Goodness knows where he got it from!"

After a couple of nights in Blackpool, the players were watching *Football Focus* on BBC TV on the Saturday, when they learned that the match at Blackburn had been called off. So they headed back to Southampton.

From the other side...

We made the mistake of thinking we had done the hard work and would have no trouble back at our place. We felt invincible at Villa Park and the ground was a stronghold.

We were a very good team in the making – Brian Little, Ray Graydon, Andy Gray and others – and we were devastated to lose, having assumed we would go through.

It was a team that won two League Cups and we couldn't believe we had failed.

You then follow the other team's progress, thinking that it could and should have been you. I find it strange these days when teams put out reserve sides in Cup competitions. We just wanted to win any competition we entered and this was one game we knew we should have won.

Chris Nicholl

Having "assumed" that Villa would win, Nicholl was still battling, deep into extra-time – the clock shows 9.45 pm – to save face. With Blyth (*left*) and Gilchrist in support, Steele is out-jumped by Nicholl (No 5).

On the march...

I don't know how many Saints fans can boast of going to every game in the Cup run but I did.

An insurance company is to blame for that. When my parents' house in Archers Road burned down in December 1975, the insurers put the whole family up in the *Gateway Hotel* in Northlands Road. John Tubbs, the hotel manager, was a fanatical Saints fan.

When he announced that he was going to drive to Villa Park, I didn't fancy it. But he talked me into accompanying him.

I was on my way to becoming one of the few.

Duncan Holley

We drove up and bought tickets on the night. We found ourselves behind the goal, in with a lot of Villa fans, some of whom were threatening us during the match. There were a lot of police mixed in, though, so they couldn't start anything.

Anyway, they left before extra-time and I imagine that's when some windows were broken on one of the Southampton coaches, a matter of concern raised by editor Malcolm Price in the next home programme.

On the way back, we got completely lost and ended up in the centre of London. A police car pulled us over and Paul, who was driving, begged us to behave as his mate had clocked him in for the night-shift at the railway works and he didn't want to get found out. They said they'd stopped us because we were driving "too carefully". It took a lot to convince them that we were heading home to Southampton from the Aston Villa match, via London.

Phil Rawlings

In other news...

There were striking similarities between then and now in terms of the major threat to London residents. In January 1976, the capital was rocked by a series of explosions in the West End. On one day, 12 bombs went off, with another failing to detonate.

Remarkably, only one person, a taxi driver, was injured. Anti-terrorist officers investigated and found that the bombs were planted in the day-time but set to explode at night, four of them outside employment agencies and another in *Selfridge's* in Oxford Street.

The IRA would later admit responsibility for the first explosions in central London for more than a year.

Perry Como topped the album charts with *40 Greatest Hits* while ITV launched its new series, *Bouquet of Barbed Wire*, starring Susan Penhaligon and Frank Finlay.

Fourth Round

The Dell   **24 January 1976**

SOUTHAMPTON 3   BLACKPOOL 1

Channon 2, Stokes   Alcock
Att: 21,553   Referee: Ron Challis

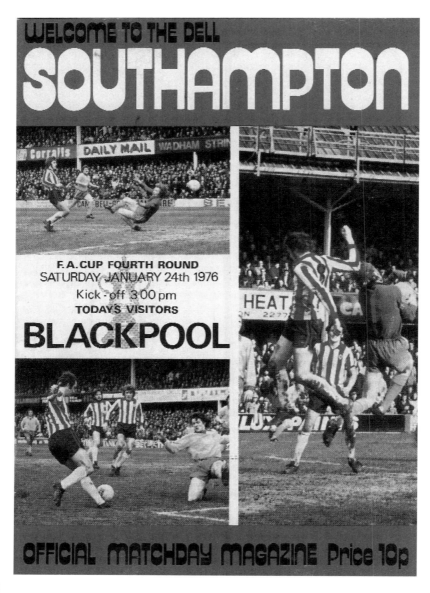

TEAM CHECK

Red & White stripes, Black shorts, White socks	CHANGES		Tangerine Shirts White Shorts	CHANGES
Ian Turner		**1**	George Wood	
Peter Rodrigues		**2**	Dave Hatton	
David Peach		**3**	Steve Harrison	
Nick Holmes		**4**	Stan McEwan	
Paul Bennett		**5**	Paul Hart	
Jim Steele		**6**	Terry Alcock	
Hugh Fisher		**7**	John Evanson	
Mike Channon		**8**	Alan Ainscow	
Peter Osgood		**9**	Mike Walsh	
Jim McCalliog		**10**	Bill Bentley	
Bobby Stokes		**11**	Jim Weston	
Paul Gilchrist		**12**		

Team Changes

SAINTS	5 Blyth	12 O'Brien
BLACKPOOL	8 Moore	12 Ronson

Highlights

1 min: Saints went close, Fisher bringing save from Wood.

5 mins: 1-0 Turner clearance to Peach, crossed to near post, for **Channon** to head into far corner past Wood
McCalliog headed just over bar.
Peach lobbed from left wing; Wood pushed over the bar.

31 mins: Turner saved twice – from Walsh; then Hatton.
Peach crudely fouled by McEwan, who was booked.
Osgood right-foot drive from 30 yds, pushed past post by Wood.
HT 1-0

56 mins: 2-0 Channon brought down by Walsh. Peach free-kick miscued by Osgood, but steered home by **Stokes**.

65 mins: Evanson's corner brought shot from Bentley; blocked but Moore tried cheeky flick just over bar.

67 mins: 3-0 Peach corner powerfully headed home by **Channon**.

88 mins: O'Brien replaced McCalliog

89 mins: 3-1 **Hatton** shot home from edge of area.
FT 3-1

When the two teams had been paired in the Third Round, two seasons before, Saints had been a First Division side and therefore shorter-odds favourites. This time they met as two Second Division sides in a game which Lawrie McMenemy was worried about. Mel Blyth recalls that,

> more than any other of the games, he wanted to get this one out of the way – which we did. The thing was we were so good at home that season: we only lost one game and drew two, in the League.

McMenemy need not have worried. They played well that day and Mick Channon's early goal gave them the confidence to go on to a convincing win. It certainly helped that the Seasiders were going through an injury crisis which, according to their manager, Harry Potts, had left them with only 13 fit players.

Ian Turner confirms Blyth's faith in their home form: "you always fancy yourself when you're at home. When you think about that season, we missed out on promotion because of our away form, but we always got results at home." For Blyth it was a swift return to action. He had picked up an injury in the Villa Park replay, which had been diagnosed as fractures to the transverse bones in the back. Don Taylor knew that there was no cure other than rest and, with the Blackburn postponement, his patient had missed only one League match, a home draw with Bolton Wanderers.

Channon opens the scoring.

As Channon (*right*) hovers for a chance, Stokes (half-hidden) stabs in Saints' second.

Blyth and Jim Steele were up against an attack which relied for its goals on Mickey Walsh, whose goal against Sunderland in the previous season's FA Cup had been the BBC "Goal of the Season". But their on-field relationship, which would prove such a key factor later in the competition, was by now really gelling, thanks to Blyth's figuring out what it required of Steele – and saying so.

> At Palace, I had been a sweeper and initially Lawrie had a problem getting someone to play alongside me. He wanted me to be the ball-winner, which I wasn't too comfortable with. But with Steelie, we could play the left/right thing. I had a long chat with him because he was in and out of the side and I knew he was a loose cannon, who wanted to do his little bits and pieces on the ball. So I said "If you want to do that, do it in front of me; so if anything does happen, I can cover it."

Hugh Fisher enjoyed playing against his former club although, his having by now been at The Dell almost nine years, there was, on the day, no-one on the other side with whom he had played. He just remembers that "we were never in danger of losing and dominated the play."

Jim McCalliog was carrying an injury and was not, he admits, having one of his better days. He was replaced by Gerry O'Brien during the second half. Somewhat the forgotten man, because he was to leave before the semi-final, O'Brien would actually make two substitute appearances during the Cup run. Blyth reckons that the players were always keen to help him – and, indeed, any other squad-member who might be on the bench – to get on and so earn his appearance money: "a few of the players would work it so someone needed to go off to get him on."

On the march...

I refused to attend this game *on principle* – the principle being the one I'd pronounced, with all the weighty authority of a 15 year-old, to my friend, Andy House, as we'd left The Dell after the draw with Villa. "We're not going to win the Cup," I'd put it to Andy, "so we might as well get knocked out sooner as later." The Saints were lying fourth in the table and we didn't want a Cup run to interfere with our promotion push, did we?

The team's performance at Villa Park showed that they had other ideas but I was not alone in my logic, as editor Malcolm Price acknowledged in the Blackpool programme. "Many people," he believed, had "mixed feelings on a good Cup run, in so much that they think that promotion prospects can suffer as a result." Yet he was "sure that this trend of thought is not shared by Manager Lawrie McMenemy and his players who like to get in a habit – that of winning."

But, then, my feelings were not mixed: I wanted us to lose, so it wouldn't have been right to be there.

Steve Eckersley

From the other side

The Saints were a favourite club for me to play against, because I always seemed to score [eight times in the three League seasons of 1974-77, in which he never failed to score at The Dell].

In fact, I'd already got a hat-trick against them that season – all in the first 25 minutes [in Blackpool's 4-3 win at Bloomfield Road].

I enjoyed playing at The Dell, but it could be an intimidating atmosphere. And, of course, Lawrie McMenemy was becoming a big name.

I became mates with Mick Channon, a couple of years later, when I was an Everton player and he was at Manchester City. Our families spent a very happy Christmas together, along with Asa Hartford. We all got snowed in.

I pinched Micky's 'windmill' celebration when I was playing in Portugal, later. And I played in South Africa with him and Mel Blyth [for Cape Town City, as seen below]. I remember that fondly – I scored five in one match.

Mickey Walsh

The Cape Town City line-up for the summer of 1978.

Back row (*left to right*): Frank Lord, Billy Anderson, Tony Sass, Patrick Wasmuth, Mick Hill, Mel Blyth, Ben Anderson, Sandy Allan.
Front: Gary France, Alan Welsh, Kevin Keegan, Mickey Walsh, John Sissons, Mick Channon.

In other news...

The trial of the "Maguire Seven" was about to get underway at the Old Bailey. Arrested on suspicion of involvement in the Guildford bombings, 40 year-old Anne Maguire, along with five family members and a close friend, would be found guilty of possessing explosives.

Mrs Maguire, from Willesden, North London, was convicted of possessing nitro-glycerine, which was then passed on to the IRA for use in making bombs, and sentenced to 14 years in prison. Her husband received the same sentence and her brother-in-law, Patrick Conlon, 12 years.

Of the seven, Patrick Conlon was the only one who didn't live to see freedom when the Court of Appeal quashed their convictions, as having been unsafe, in 1991. His story was central to the subsequent Oscar-winning film, The Sins of the Father.

In February 2005, Prime Minister Tony Blair issued a public apology to The Maguire Seven *and* The Guildford Four *for the miscarriage of justice they had suffered.*

Ferrari driver Nikki Lauda won the first Formula 1 Grand Prix of the season in Brazil.

The BBC banned Donna Summer's *Love To Love You Baby*, which contained heavy breathing and sounds of simulated love-making, for being 'too sexy'. Meanwhile, Abba were Number 1 in the charts with *Mamma Mia*.

On television's *That's Life*, Esther Rantzen uncovered London's happiest bus conductor – all-singing, all-dancing Andy Melish.

In respect of the next four rounds, a few of the quoted recollections are from interviews for previous publications. Thus Rodrigues, on his signing (page 28); Rodrigues and McMenemy, on scouting reports (page 75); and Channon, on ceding the captaincy (page 107), are from *Dell Diamond* interviews, while the thoughts of Rodrigues on there being "something on" (page 30) are from Chris Newman's 1996 interview. The Wembley memories of Gerry Daly and Lou Macari (pages 94 and 96) are from a TV interview and an autobiography, respectively. For details of these publications, see "Sources" at the end of the book.

Fifth Round

The Hawthorns   **14 February 1976**

WEST BROMWICH ALBION 1   SOUTHAMPTON 1

Brown   Stokes

Att: 36,634   Referee: Clive Thomas

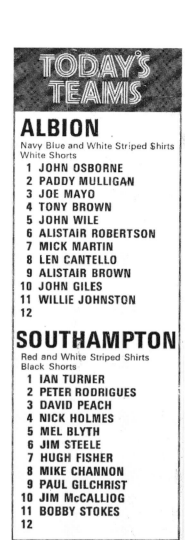

TODAY'S TEAMS

ALBION
Navy Blue and White Striped Shirts
White Shorts
1 JOHN OSBORNE
2 PADDY MULLIGAN
3 JOE MAYO
4 TONY BROWN
5 JOHN WILE
6 ALISTAIR ROBERTSON
7 MICK MARTIN
8 LEN CANTELLO
9 ALISTAIR BROWN
10 JOHN GILES
11 WILLIE JOHNSTON
12

SOUTHAMPTON
Red and White Striped Shirts
Black Shorts
1 IAN TURNER
2 PETER RODRIGUES
3 DAVID PEACH
4 NICK HOLMES
5 MEL BLYTH
6 JIM STEELE
7 HUGH FISHER
8 MIKE CHANNON
9 PAUL GILCHRIST
10 JIM McCALLIOG
11 BOBBY STOKES
12

Highlights

Osgood suspended; replaced by Gilchrist. Saints camp hit by bug. Wile soon booked for bringing Channon down.

12 mins: Turner misjudged Martin's cross, which hit far post.

15 mins: Peach corner to near post; Steele, racing in, headed just wide of far post.

Saints' 12-pass move ended with McCalliog's shot blocked by Martin.

35 mins: Peach booked for a second foul on Johnston.

Just before half-time, Channon's header parried by Osborne; hooked off line by Mulligan.

HT 0-0

58 mins: 0-1 Johnston's cross from by-line turned in by **Tony Brown** from 12 yds.

Osborne dropped ball at feet of Stokes, who hooked over bar

75 mins: 1-1 Channon laid back, for **Stokes** to steer inside Osborne's right-hand post.

Turner turned Robertson's shot over bar.

Final five minutes; Alistair Brown headed against post.

FT 1-1

Team Changes

WBA	12 Robson
SAINTS	12 Earles

Although he dismisses such suggestions, most of the side reckon that Mick Channon was the first of the players to get the feeling that this might be their year. This was the round and the game when a couple of his team-mates – Ian Turner and Paul Gilchrist – started to share his optimism.

For Turner, it wasn't so much a case of believing the Twin Towers were beckoning than sensing "a nice Cup run" was in the offing. For him, the moment that he saw as fate was when a late header from West Brom striker Alistair Brown went past him, hit the post, but, as he "turned round, it just landed in my arms."

As much as the glory of the Cup, Turner realised that going on a run would have a very pleasant financial benefit.

It counted in your pocket, because the bonus would increase with every round. Appearance money was the same but, whereas the win-bonus might have been £20 in the beginning, it started to climb, as we went through the rounds, to £50 then £100 – and so on.

Any prospect of a win-bonus must have seemed remote on the morning of the game with Mick Channon, Bobby Stokes and Nick Holmes all suffering from upset stomachs. Hugh Fisher remembers, in particular, that Stokes was really poorly on the morning of the match.

In fact, a few guys were on their knees. We had a small squad and there was only one substitute allowed, so we were up against it. We were under the cosh in the first half, but we battled hard to get back into it and earn a replay.

The days of squads of 16 or more travelling to a match were a long way in the future, so there was nothing for it but to try and struggle through. And struggle they did! Channon remembers Holmes as "probably the fittest player we ever had." At one point, Mick had drifted wide when he "heard someone coming up outside me, wheezing and breathing really heavily, like a steam train. I wondered what was going on and looked across to see Nick really struggling. The tummy bug was having an effect and for Nick to struggle was really something."

As Channon demands maximum attention,
a "wheezing" Holmes labours to his aid.

Willie Johnston had been a constant thorn in the side that afternoon, to the extent that Saints' best player, David Peach, was booked by Clive Thomas for taking his attempts to stop him a little too far.

Putting aside the effects of illness, and despite now going a goal down, Saints were potentially able to draw confidence from their recent record against Albion: since dropping back into Division II, they had beaten them on each of the four occasions they had met. The home team may have been fifth in the table – and, as it turned out, on their way to promotion – but with Channon leading the line, the visitors pushed forward with even greater urgency.

From Channon's lay-back, Stokes steers Saints level.

Given Fisher's bulletin on Stokes's ill-health, for Bobby to score the equaliser was a great credit to his resilience. And there will be plenty of Saints fans who remember the quality of the goal, as the crowd of over 36,000 is estimated to have contained a travelling support of around 10,000.

Paul Gilchrist admits to having been more nervous at The Hawthorns than anywhere. Previously, he had only ever experienced the early rounds of the Cup.

> I knew if we won we would be getting quite close. We played quite well, Bobby scored a great goal and we hung on. It was probably the start of the momentum with things going our way. The players were starting to enjoy it and I thought "this is good, this."

Jim McCalliog's memories of the tie have more to do with his personal battle, in midfield, with Johnny Giles, whom he greatly admired. West Brom's player-manager may have been 35 years-old, but he was still a handful: "he was a smashing player and I had a busy day."

Thirteen years previously, Giles had been a member of the Manchester United side that beat the Saints in the semi-final before going on to win the Cup. But McCalliog felt he still had a lot to offer and might usefully have stayed in the game longer than he did: so much of what he had to say about football was "spot-on".

Giles, the midfield-general so admired by McCalliog, obscures Clive Thomas's view of a heading duel between Steele and Mayo.

The last word on that Valentine's Day trip to the West Midlands goes to the skipper. If Gilchrist and Turner were starting to look a little further forward, Peter Rodrigues still had his feet planted firmly on the ground. As far as he was concerned, Saints had "nicked a draw. I certainly wasn't thinking of Wembley. It was just a relief that we got a result."

It was a result that set the stage for one of those special midweek floodlit games at The Dell.

On the march...

I had turned 16 in January and was due to leave school in May/June. I agreed with the careers teacher that I'd try all the big local employers for an apprenticeship. He informed me that one of them – British Rail Works – had an Open Day coming up and would I like to put my name down to attend? Of course I would.

Meanwhile, my school-mate, Mike Godwin, had booked our tickets on the "Football Special" train to West Bromwich and we were ready to go. Or so I thought – until I discovered that the Open Day was Saturday 14 February. There was no choice: I just had to tell my careers teacher I was going to football. He was not impressed. "What are you thinking: you'd turn down a job opportunity to go and watch Saints play?" "Yes". I didn't see a problem.

So he marched me off to see the Head. "This boy intends to go and watch a football match, rather than attend the British Rail Open Day." The Head then lectured me, for what seemed an eternity, before he, in his turn, asked me to choose. I still chose football and the school's support for my future career ended that day.

But, hey, I was on that train and on my way to joining the biggest gathering of away supporters I'd yet seen. Bobby Stokes equalised in the goal right in front of us. Once the celebrations had finished, I seemed to be closer to the pitch then when they started. Oh for those days of standing on the terraces!

By the way, I got an apprenticeship. At Vosper Thornycroft.
Dave Webster

I was watching Saints 'A' at BAT Totton, in the Hampshire League, Division II. With the first-team trailing at The Hawthorns and the 'A's down 2-0 at half-time, Tony Sealy – who would, of course, come on at Wembley in the Saints' next Final, in 1979 – pulled one back. A little later, news filtered through that Bobby Stokes had equalised at West Brom. The 'A' team never did equalise.
Brian Saunders

It was my 600th game in total. And I do remember Willie Johnston pulling the ball back to me. I just helped it in.
Tony Brown

Note: *Anyone who holds his club record for League appearances (574) and goals (218) is surely entitled to forget the details of a Cup-tie in which he scored a routine goal, albeit in a milestone game.*

In other news...
In another parallel with 2006, Britain had a Labour Prime Minister coming to the end of an extended period in office.

After leading the Labour Party for 13 years, Harold Wilson was entering his last month in office. With his 60th birthday approaching, Wilson, who had spent almost eight years at 10 Downing Street, would announce his resignation and stun the country and the political world.

Altogether, Wilson had been an MP for 31 years, having been, at 31, the youngest Cabinet Minister since William Pitt the Younger. He revealed he had decided to resign two years before. He had informed the Queen the previous December, but the story hadn't leaked and he told a shocked Cabinet, "I have not wavered in this decision and it is irrevocable."

American DJ, Emperor Rosko, left Radio 1 after eight years on the station and was replaced by Canadian DJ, "Kid" Jensen. It wouldn't be long before he would echo Ray Wilkins's efforts to drop the "Butch", when he stopped answering to "Kid" and insisted on being called David.

Midge Ure's band Slik went to Number 1 on the singles chart with *Forever And Ever* and the top album was *The Very Best Of Slim Whitman*.

On TV, John McEnery and Jane Seymour starred in ITV's *Our Mutual Friend*.

Fifth Round replay

The Dell   **17 February 1976**

SOUTHAMPTON 4   **WEST BROMWICH ALBION 0**

Channon 3 (1 pen), Gilchrist

Att: 27,614   Referee: Alf Gray

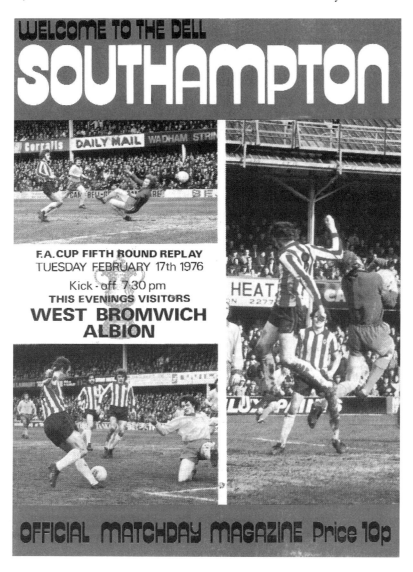

TEAM CHECK

SAINTS

Red & White stripes, Black shorts, White socks

	CHANGES			CHANGES
Ian Turner		**1**		
Peter Rodrigues		**2**		
David Peach		**3**		
Nick Holmes		**4**		
Mel Blyth		**5**		
Jim Steele		**6**		
Hugh Fisher		**7**		
Mike Channon		**8**		
Paul Gilchrist		**9**		
Jim McCalliog		**10**		
Bobby Stokes		**11**		
		12		

ALBION

Yellow shirts, Green shorts

	CHANGES
John Osborne	
Paddy Mulligan	
Joe Mayo	
Tony Brown	
John Wile	
Alistair Robertson	
Mick Martin	
Len Cantello	
Alistair Brown	
John Giles	
Willie Johnston	

Team Changes

SAINTS   12 O'Brien
WBA   12 Robson

Highlights

Saints' biggest crowd of season and record receipts.

1 min: 1-0 **Channon** played one-two with Stokes, before placing shot in far corner.

West Brom should have levelled when Peach chipped back-pass over Turner but A. Brown handled.

17 mins: 2-0 Stokes's shot rebounded to **Gilchrist**, who flicked ball up and shot home over his shoulder.

WBA should have cut gap when Johnston took Mayo's through ball past Turner but hit shot against Blyth

30 mins: 3-0 **Channon** took pass from Peach and rounded Osborne to score.

HT 3-0

Bryan Robson replaced A. Brown
Turner saved well from T. Brown twice.

74 mins: 4-0 **Channon** pen after he was pushed in back by Wile.

78 mins O'Brien replaced Stokes

85 mins: Cantello put Robertson clear but he froze with only Turner to beat.

FT 4-0

If you're old enough to remember the Cup run recounted in this book, then it's a fair bet that your treasure-trove of Saints memories includes quite a few floodlit evenings at The Dell. The 1976 squad clearly share your nostalgic affection and this game was, as Nick Holmes recalls, "special, under the lights: they seemed to give us an extra yard."

And given a yard, the Saints on this occasion took a mile. All of those who played in this replay think of it as one of their finest performances. Which meant a quiet evening for Ian Turner in goal: "we were brilliant that night. We tore them apart and were completely comfortable. I don't think I had anything to do."

Steve Middleton had started the season as first-choice 'keeper and Turner had regained the green jersey only at the end of November. By now confident of his place and his form, he was also in a good position to judge the team-mates in front of him: this was a side of "bread-and-butter players," complemented by star-performers in Channon, Osgood, McCalliog and Rodrigues, who "had been about and helped and encouraged everyone." It all added up, Turner reckoned, to "a good team who encouraged each other and stuck by each other."

One of the key performers for the home team was David Peach. He again faced Scottish international Willie Johnston but, whereas on the Saturday the winger had created Albion's goal and generally given the Saints plenty of problems, this time Peach was dominant. It helped, he feels, that the visitors "didn't like it because of the crowd getting the atmosphere going. I had a pretty good relationship with the fans, which probably sprang from me making a good start with the club."

He had scored in his second start in February 1974 – a 3-1 win against Newcastle. With Brian O'Neil out for a cartilage operation, that was one of the occasions when Peach played in midfield. But he initially had cause to wonder just what role McMenemy had in mind for him.

> The day after I signed, I went to Bristol with Lawrie to watch the England Under-23s and Steve Mills was playing left-back. He was different class and I asked Lawrie why he had signed me. He said he was going to play Steve at right-back and me at left-back.

That happened a few times before Mills was seriously injured in a car accident a year later. Although he tried a number of comebacks, Steve never fully recovered. During the 1975 close season, McMenemy brought in Peter Rodrigues on a free transfer from Sheffield Wednesday – "as a bit of a stop-gap," the player assumed, yet he came into this replay not having missed a game all season.

Peter Osgood was completing a two-match suspension, so Paul Gilchrist kept the No. 9 shirt. It was as a striker that he had come south from Doncaster.

> When I left Charlton I dropped to the Fourth Division and signed for Maurice Setters at Doncaster. Going down a couple of divisions gave me the confidence to play better. I loved it there but it was quite basic, fish and chips after the game and so forth. Then I came to the Saints, which was a big step back up.

Jim Steele had just arrived and Gilchrist found a dressing room full of characters. It always amuses him to remember his arrival at The Dell in 1972, when a local taxi-driver was quick to tell him his fortune.

> Of course, I was behind Ron Davies and Mick Channon for a starting place. I was really bought as back-up to them. I remember getting a taxi to the ground when I came to sign and the taxi-driver told me I had no chance of getting in the team as a centre-forward, with Ron there.

Having flicked the ball up, Gilchrist volleys it over his shoulder for the Saints' second.

So, although by now Saints fans had become used to Gilchrist playing on the right of a midfield three, he was quite capable of a striking role – as he proved in memorable fashion with a spectacular overhead kick for the second goal of the night: "This was probably the best we played. They were a good side and hard to beat, but in the first half it was one of those incredible nights at The Dell. My goal was one I do remember."

Despite the satisfaction of a job well done, Jim Steele believes it was a night that typified the season.

> We were brilliant at home but we couldn't play away, which is why we weren't promoted – that and having our minds on the Cup. I used to get so upset because we should have hammered every team in that League and walked straight back up.

Nick Holmes had the assignment that had stretched Jim McCalliog at The Hawthorns: it was his turn to mark Johnny Giles.

> He was a tough character. A good footballer and everything went through him. Probably one of the best I had played against at that stage in my career. Having said that, you always knew with that type of player that they would be limited in their defensive duties; so if you could close them down, they would give you a chance going the other way.

Mick Channon and Hugh Fisher were the only survivors of the side that had lost to West Brom in a Fourth Round replay in 1968. Fisher, so far ever-present in this 1976 Cup run, sums up the performance.

> Channon was electric. I just remember him running past people and scoring. The team spirit really shone through, that night, and we were on a roll. The work ethic was really good, we were sharp and we worked well as a unit.

On a roll? Holmes thinks "it was probably there that we started feeling it could be our year." And even Rodrigues, feet still rooted after the draw at The Hawthorns, admits that he was now beginning to think "there may be something on here."

The first two-thirds of Channon's hat-trick

Above: He opens the scoring in the first minute.

Below: Having left goalkeeper Osborne on his knees, he slides in his second, and Saints' third, on the half-hour.

From the other side…

We were awful, which is probably why I can't remember much about the match. I remember more of winning at The Dell on the way to winning the Cup in 1968.

I do remember I had the flu [in 1976] and that Bryan Robson, who was only 19, was substitute. He was a young lad with so much confidence yet so slight. They were building him up with sherry and steaks and eggs – him and Asa Hartford. We all knew he was going to be a very good player. A very confident young lad who would think nothing of giving the older players a rollicking.

I hated playing at The Dell. It felt like the crowd were on top of you. It was very intimidating and I never enjoyed playing there.

Tony Brown

In other news...

Harold Wilson had resigned from a Government that held no majority and the resignation from the Labour Party of former Cabinet Minister John Stonehouse, a few weeks later, would leave them with a minority of one.

Stonehouse, who came from Southampton, was MP for Walsall North and had faked his own death by staging an apparent drowning off a beach in Miami in November 1974. He was arrested, five weeks later, in Melbourne, Australia.

In the court case that would follow his demise as a politician, his secretary, Sheila Buckley, and he would face 18 charges of theft, forgery, attempted insurance frauds and conspiracy, involving more than £170,000. Stonehouse would be convicted and sentenced to seven years in prison, while Buckley would receive a suspended two-year sentence. He would be released in 1979 on health grounds; marry Buckley in 1981; and die of a heart attack, aged 62, in 1988.

On television, the first series of *Space 1999* continued, with the episode, "The Infernal Machine".

The Four Seasons were on their way to Number 1 with *December '63 (Oh What A Night).*

Sixth Round

Valley Parade   **6 March 1976**

BRADFORD CITY 0   SOUTHAMPTON 1

Att: 14,195

McCalliog
Referee: Bob Matthewson

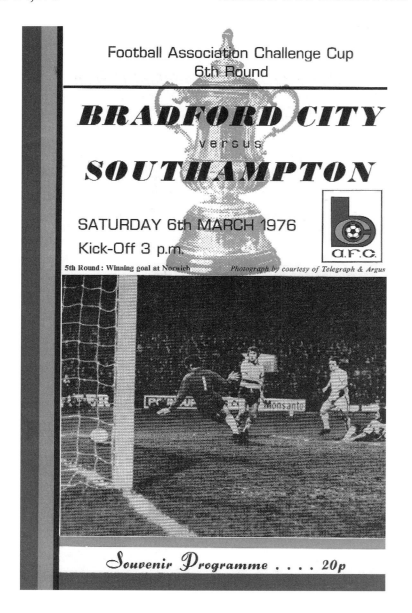

Football Association Challenge Cup
6th Round

BRADFORD CITY
versus
SOUTHAMPTON

SATURDAY 6th MARCH 1976
Kick-Off 3 p.m.

5th Round : Winning goal at Norwich

Photograph by courtesy of Telegraph & Argus

b.
a.f.c.

Souvenir Programme 20p

BRADFORD CITY		SOUTHAMPTON
(Amber Shirts, Claret Shorts)	**Referee:** R. MATTHEWSON (Bolton)	(Gold Shirts and Blue Shorts)
1 DOWNSBOROUGH, P		1 TURNER, Ian
2 PODD, Cyril		2 RODRIGUES, Peter
3 COOPER, Ian	For all Electronic Components Hi-Fi & Recording accessories phone 24008	3 PEACH, David
4 JOHNSON, Rod		4 HOLMES, Micky
5 MIDDLETON, John	CENTRAL RADIO	5 BLYTHE, Mel
6 FRETWELL, David	(B R A D F O R D)	6 STEELE, Jim
7 McGINLEY, Billy	93 KIRKGATE BRADFORD	7 FISHER, Hugh
8 INGRAM, Gerry		8 CHANNON, Mike
9 COOKE, Joe	**Linesmen:** Orange Flag	9 GILCHRIST, Paul
10 HALL, David	N. MIDGLEY (Salford)	10 McCALLIOG, Jim
11 HUTCHINS, Don	Red Flag	11 STOKES, Bobby
12 HOCKEY, Trevor	J. B. WORRALL (Warrington)	12 OSGOOD, Peter

Records Loaned by VALLANCES, MARKET STREET, BRADFORD

Team Changes

BRADFORD No changes
SAINTS 4 Gilchrist 6 Bennett 9 Osgood 12 O'Brien

Highlights

Steele (mumps) and Holmes (training injury) miss their only game of run, while Bennett becomes the 13th man to start in it.
England boss Don Revie watching Channon.
Stokes passed to Gilchrist, who shot over from 25 yds.
Bradford had more of the early attacks.
Referee spoke to Cooke after he went in strongly on Turner.
20 mins: Peach, then Stokes and Channon, fashioned a chance for Fisher who forced a diving save from Downsborough.
29 mins: Ingram beat Peach to cross, but Hutchins shot high and wide.
Stokes's forward pass came off Cooper's head but Channon shot over bar.
41 mins: 1-0 Gilchrist tripped by Fretwell. Osgood flicked free-kick up for **McCalliog**, who volleyed past Downsborough.
Bradford nearly equalised, but Turner saved brilliantly from Johnson.
HT 1-0

Osgood headed McCalliog's corner down, but Channon couldn't reach before Johnson cleared.
Bradford's Middleton and McCalliog both booked.
Channon caught a boot in the face from Middleton; while he was down, Rodrigues shot but Downsborough turned behind.
Turner saved twice after poor back-passes.
Last few minutes played in Saints' half.
FT 1-0

After winning their way through to the Sixth Round, the Saints had to wait a week to see whether they would be travelling to First Division Norwich City or Fourth Division Bradford City, whose Fifth Round tie at Carrow Road had been twice postponed because of a flu epidemic in the Bradford camp.

If Saints fans were assuming that the next Cup away-day would be to East Anglia, the players were no different. And it wasn't an attractive prospect: "Carrow Road was a place we never won at," Paul Gilchrist recollects – in fact, the Saints had never even scored there since he'd been at the club – "so we were delighted that Bradford got through." They mostly were, indeed. Nick Holmes "can remember when the result came through."

> I started thinking that we could beat Bradford and be in the semi-finals. It really got home to me because everyone expected that we would be playing Norwich. It seemed like everything was falling into place for us.

Hugh Fisher likewise recalls how the players "did get quite excited. Mick Channon called me, at about 10.30 at night, shouting about Bradford winning and saying 'we can beat them.' As far as he was concerned, we were already at Wembley."

Jim Clunie (*top*), Fisher and Holmes have boarded the bus for the airport (and the flight to Bradford), while some of the party make a fashion statement.
Gilchrist (*left*), having played in Yorkshire, has dressed for a drop in temperature – to the apparent disdain of Yorkshire-born Turner (next to him). The others – O'Brien, Peach, Rodrigues, Bennett and Earles – are content to display their checks and flairs.

Yet it was anything but a formality. Although the team was by now fairly settled, this match was the only one in the run in which any alteration was needed to the defensive line-up. This was because Jim Steele was suffering from the mumps. Left behind, he found the suspense almost unbearable: "I walked around Southampton with a big scarf on. I kept watching the TVs in the High Street shop windows and I couldn't bear it, because every time I looked, it was still nothing-each."

Steele's place was taken by Paul Bennett who had joined the club upon leaving Tauntons School in 1968. Inheriting John McGrath's No.5 shirt in October 1972, he had made it his for most of the next three years – with Blyth and Steele beginning to establish a regular partnership only in December 1975. If there were no reason, then, to be concerned about the capabilities of Steele's deputy, it would require a change of approach from Mel Blyth: "Paul was an out-and-out centre-half. Obviously, I had to do things differently to what I was used to with Jim, but Paul played really well."

Holmes also missed the match – in most frustrating circumstances. The party flew north on the Thursday morning. Once they had settled in their hotel, they went for a training session and, within five minutes, Holmes had twisted his knee.

> I felt terrible. I kept thinking it would be all right but those two days up there were hard work for me. All the lads were buzzing, playing table tennis, cards and so on. I played table tennis to try and be a part of it all, which probably made the injury worse.

He watched the game from the stand with Pat Earles, while Gerry O'Brien, the 14th member of the party, sat on the bench. O'Brien – who claims to have been the person who nicknamed Peter Rodrigues "Pedro" – didn't get on and would be transferred to Swindon within the week. While he appreciated the goal as "one of the best," Holmes found it hard to be a spectator.

> All of a sudden I had doubt. It was an injury that I hadn't experienced before. How long was I going to be out? Was I going to be ready for the next game? Although it was great to get through, I was wondering if I would miss the next round.

Once again, Ian Turner took his inspiration from the disparaging comments of others. The previous Saturday, the Saints had lost at York – their first defeat since November – and their (non-playing) centre-forward, Jimmy Seal, had said they weren't a good side and they couldn't compete: "he really wound us up. We went to Bradford confident, but not over-confident, that we could battle it."

And battle it, they did, demonstrating that, contrary to Seal's prediction, they could *compete*. But, then, Turner knew what it was like to compete at this level. And so did David Peach, who found Bradford "a typical Fourth Division side, who rolled their sleeves up and didn't care about reputations. They got their heads down and we did struggle, but our back four defended well; and then the magic from Ossie and Jim got us through."

Turner had the last laugh, moreover, with a late save that featured in *Match of the Day*'s "Save of the Season". The goal that won the game is not one that has been relentlessly shown by the BBC, but the Saints fans who have a copy of the *Match of the Day: Southampton FC* video, on which the goal is replayed, probably outnumber those who were there, on the day, to witness the "magic". If many more carry a mental image of it, that is no doubt due in part to its oral history – an inventive manoeuvre, it has been much described – but also because, unlike some of the 11 other goals that the run had so far yielded, a fine original photo of this magic moment has been preserved in the *Echo* archives and reproduced in "Souvenir" editions.

Having served his two-match suspension, Peter Osgood was on hand, when a free-kick was won on the edge of the Bradford penalty area, to respond to Jim McCalliog's unusual request.

> We had done it a few times in training, just clowning about. I told Ossie to flick it up and he just said "What?" I repeated it and he lifted it and I hit it sweet as a nut. I didn't even look. As soon as I hit it, I knew it was in and I ran to the side and did a highland jig or something. I don't know what I was doing, really. It was an exciting thing.

While acknowledging this "great goal", Mick Channon dismisses any suggestion of its resulting from training-ground preparation: "it certainly was not rehearsed. But, then, none of us ever knew what anyone was going to do – which was our strength, as well as our weakness."

Having flicked the ball up, Osgood watches nonchalantly, hands on hips,
as McCalliog volleys it over the wall to score.

It seems that, among those Bradford fans prepared to concede that it was ever a free-kick in the first place, there are those who question, to this day, the validity of Osgood's delivery. Their case rests, apparently, on the celebrated Carr-Hunt precedent. Older fans may recall that famous televised free-kick, in 1970, when Coventry's Willie Carr flicked the ball up, from between his heels, for Ernie Hunt to volley home. The goal not only stood but was voted *Match of the Day* "Goal of the Season". Even so, the practice was duly outlawed, Carr being deemed to have played the ball twice, once with each heel, although it is alternatively argued, in some circles, that the ball had not travelled its circumference.

Either way, the referee deemed Osgood's flick within the rules – which is just as well, given that this might fairly be said to have been the only exciting moment in a thoroughly drab affair. Bennett had anticipated "a dour game. It might as well have been Siberia for us, firstly because it was against a lower division side and secondly because anything north of the Watford Gap was foreign territory in those days."

Others shared Blyth's verdict on Paul's performance. Peter Rodrigues appreciated that Bennett "did well", slotting into a defence that worked the offside trap and the rest, as a unit in which they "all knew what each other would do." Of the three players who appeared in the Cup run but who would not receive a medal, Paul was the only one to play an entire match. A modest man, he "always believed" that his duties as the marker were the "simple" part of central-defending.

> You knew your job was to stick to your man. The players who swept round –
> Jim Steele, David Walker, Jimmy Gabriel – they were the thinkers of the game.
> For me, it was marking; and I would say the hardest to mark were Jimmy Greaves,
> Ted MacDougall and, the absolute best, Kenny Dalglish.

Bradford didn't have any strikers of that calibre but the pairing of Joe Cooke – a 21 year-old from the Dominican Republic, who had come through the Bantams' ranks – and the experienced Gerry Ingram had been scoring freely.

Bennett had to stop Cooke:

> My role was always to dominate the man I was marking. If he dominated me, I was no use to my team but, if I took care of him, my job was done. On this day, I did my job because they didn't score.

Valley Parade was only three-quarters full and the crowd of 14,195 was the smallest for a quarter-final since the War. The low turn-out was undoubtedly due, at least in part, to the attempt by

The Saints' centre-backs keep it tight. While Blyth towers above Ingram, Bennett (*right*) is hard at the heels of Cooke.

Bradford's Chairman, Bob Martin, to capitalise on his club's first-ever appearance in the Sixth Round.

Ticket prices were hiked by a huge margin. Terrace admission rose from 65p to £1.50, while seats trebled from £1 to £3.

Martin had considered the option of switching the match to Elland Road, nine miles away. A gate of 50,000 would have been possible there, which would have allowed him to keep ticket prices at their normal levels. But he was concerned that moving just that short distance from home "would be to hand the match to Southampton."

The Southampton board objected to the price increases, but the FA ruled in Bradford's favour. Southampton MP, Bob Mitchell, also raised the question with the Price Commission but was told that Bradford had not broken the Price Code: football clubs were regarded as service enterprises, in which it was normal custom, the Commission reasoned, to raise prices for special occasions.

In the event, Martin's gamble – that his team would become the first Fourth Division side to reach a semi-final and earn enough in the process to eliminate an £80,000 overdraft – failed. The Saints sold only 3,500 of their 5,000 allocated tickets, doubtless owing to a combination of economics and geography – although it seemed that some of those who fancied the trip assumed that the allocation was bound to sell out and so didn't even try to buy tickets. Peter Rodrigues appreciated the support of those who made it: "I was totally aware that we had a bunch of fans behind the goal who had come all that way to watch us and it certainly helped."

Having begun, after the thrashing of West Brom, "to reflect on the luck we had already had and thinking it might be our year," he differed from those who considered Bradford's win at Norwich to be a continuation of that luck.

> Actually, I didn't want Bradford because I knew it would be hard. Not a game to look forward to, because the skills of Osgood, Channon, McCalliog etc wouldn't be to the fore: it would be a battle. We wanted to get a result and maybe bring them back to The Dell. We knew it would be dour so it was a great result.

A result for McMenemy's man-management. Like so many others, Rodrigues pays tribute to the way Lawrie would "give you instructions, but every individual was treated as he needed to be. Channon and Osgood, of course, were different. You couldn't tell them how to play – thank goodness!"

The goal-scorer, McCalliog, missed the post-match celebrations with his team-mates, as they travelled back by train with their fans. He had been permitted to spend the weekend in Manchester and he left Bradford a happy man.

Lawrie had got the balance of the team right and, although we weren't playing so well in League matches, when it came to the Cup, we had that skip in our step. I was always one for taking each match in turn, but Mick Channon was actually thinking more about football than racing – which I thought must be a good thing.

Having scored a hat-trick in the previous round, Channon was now "thinking more about football than racing." But it looks as though the referee's whistle has halted his attempt to get on the score-sheet again.

On the march...
I wasn't able to go. So I listened to the scores on my faithful tranny, while watching Amesbury play on the local Rec'.

I remember the interview with McMenemy after the game and how he bemoaned the lack of passion among Saints fans. We had just reached the semi-final for the first time in 13 years and yet he had been greeted with the remark: "you made hard work of that!" "In the North East," he said, "they'd be dancing in the streets." A lady later wrote to tell him that "the difference down here is that we don't dance in the street; we dance in our kitchens."
Steve Eckersley

I remember the Bradford team getting off their coach in their impressive blazers. Vic Feather, the former General Secretary of the TUC and a life-long Bradford supporter, was with them. The crowd was swirling round the ground and, as I went towards it, I noticed some of the Southampton players standing outside, on a sort of platform, watching the crowd. I went over, held up my programme – this is me as an adult – and, sure enough, Mick Channon and Ian Turner both signed it. Imagine that: players almost in the crowd, before a big match. Can't imagine that happening now. I was right behind the free-kick for the goal and wondered then – and still wonder – if it was legal. But did we care?
Andrew Wrigley

Bradford's Cooke and Middleton (*right*) pursue the ball, watched by two Southampton players for whom this game represented contrasting fortunes. Osgood (*to the fore*) had missed three of the five games up to now – and been replaced in one of the two he had started – but was now in for the duration. On the other hand, Fisher, having been ever-present so far, would succumb to an injury he had been carrying and become a non-playing sub hereafter.

From the other side…

We beat Norwich to get to the Sixth Round and the excitement was mounting in Bradford. In hindsight you see it differently. People told us to enjoy it but, actually, the enjoyment comes from how others remember the occasion.

Of course, Southampton had a better standard of players than us, but the Cup tends to equalise those factors on the day, with the atmosphere it generates. It was close and an excellent goal decided it. If we had won, we would have even fancied our chances of getting to the Final, which would have been remarkable for a Fourth Division side.

My opposite No.9 was Peter Osgood, but I didn't worry about reputations. I was a kid and just went out there to play without any fear: that probably comes later in your career. His ability was high but you tended to meet more aggressive players in the lower divisions. We were obviously disappointed but we did give a good account of ourselves.

The bigger disappointment was looking at the semi-final draw and realising we could have had a real chance of making the Final, with Palace only being one level above us. I watched the whole day's coverage of the Final and, of course, saw our match in the highlights of the previous rounds. I wanted Saints to win on the day. I suppose mentally you can then say: if we had won our match, we could have won the Cup.

Joe Cooke

On the march...

As for my trip to the Third Round replay (previously explained), I found a chauffeur at the *Gateway Hotel*. Dave was a lad from near Bradford, who was relocating to the Southampton area with his job and was staying in the hotel, pending finding accommodation where his family would join him. He imposed one condition to taking me and three friends in his company car: his wife was not to find out he was returning to the area on a weekend when, instead of visiting her, he would be taking us to the match.

Walking to the ground at about half-past-two, we found ourselves in the middle of a hail of missiles. Dave – perhaps feeling duty-bound to protect his friends from the south – decided to "return" one such brick and was promptly pounced upon by some of Yorkshire's finest constables and hauled off to a police van. Aghast at this injustice, two of my friends tried to remonstrate. You've guessed it: before you could say "Bobby Stokes", they too were inside the van. Mark – the only other guy left – and I scampered off to the game. The atmosphere inside the ground was intimidating, too, so by the time the final whistle blew, I was anxious to get out of Bradford in one piece, especially as we had managed to nick a win and the home fans were looking pretty peeved. There was, of course, one small problem: our driver and car keys were in a Bradford police station. Cautiously, Mark and I made our way there, to see whether we could retrieve Dave or, failing that, his keys. The answers were "No!" and "No!"

So we headed for the railway station. The south-bound trains had by now gone and the platform was deserted – until a group of menacing Bradford fans appeared and, all of a sudden, there was a flurry of blows raining down on our heads and bodies. There was no option: Mark and I jumped onto the railway line and hotfooted it away as quickly as possible. We ran for about a mile, climbed over a couple of fences and found ourselves outside Valley Parade once again. The streets, too, were now deserted. It was snowing. I felt a long way from home.

The good news is that we came upon four blokes, one of whom I recognised from Southampton, who kindly gave us a lift home. The bad news is that their car was small, so I had to endure the whole drive back with Mark on my knee, bent double. What with all the bruises from the assault at the station, it was the longest and most painful return journey I have ever made from an away match but, with my first semi-final to look forward to, I was past caring.

Dave was charged and his case was all over the local papers, so his wife found out. Needless to say, she was not happy – although she did move to Southampton before they divorced. I have always felt a bit guilty that, through me, Dave found himself locked up in Bradford instead of spending time with his wife. Fortunately, his employers never discovered either his misuse of their car or his indiscretion on the streets of Bradford. So we were able to requisition his car for further expeditions.

Duncan Holley

Royal marriages in crisis don't create such headlines today as they did in 1976. The first of many was announced by Buckingham Palace in March when Princess Margaret and Lord Snowdon separated after 16 years of marriage.

Lord Snowdon was in Australia to open an exhibition of his photographic work and, at the time, was reported to have known nothing of the announcement prior to its release. He appealed for understanding for the couple's children, 14 year-old Viscount Linley and Lady Sarah Armstrong-Jones, who was 11.

Although the official announcement said there were no plans for the couple to divorce, within two years a decree nisi had been granted. Subsequently, he would marry Lucy Lindsay-Hogg but that marriage would also end in divorce in 2000. Rumours of Princess Margaret's relationship with Roddy Llewellyn, 16 years her junior at 29, had preceded the break-up and, although that relationship would continue for several years, she would never remarry.

The *TV Times* proudly announced that the Angels were back on the wards, while Nikki Lauda continued to set the pace in Formula 1, winning the second Grand Prix of the season in South Africa.

The new No.1 on the singles chart was *I Love To Love (But My Baby Just Loves To Dance)* by Tina Charles.

Semi-final Draw

Mel Blyth was confident that the Saints would be drawn against his former club: "after we beat Bradford, I always knew we were going to get Palace."

You can see why his team-mates hoped he would be proved right. Crystal Palace were in the Third Division. True, they had led that division until the end of January and were currently lying third, but the other sides in the draw were all from the top flight. Wolves were only one place off the bottom of the First Division, but they had forced a draw at Old Trafford. So third-placed Manchester United were facing a replay at Molineux. The fourth ball waiting to be drawn was that of Derby County, the 1975 League Champions, who were lying one place behind United.

The Southampton players gathered in their dressing-room, on the Monday lunch-time, with a portable radio tuned to BBC Radio 2. They heard the FA Secretary, Ted Croker, say

Derby County will play… Manchester United or Wolv……

The rest was lost in the cacophony of noise that erupted – as can be seen *opposite*. Paul Gilchrist, a confirmed pessimist, had "expected the hard draw, but getting Palace was great for us – although they were a tough side, so we weren't taking them for granted." Indeed, not – even Mick Channon, for all his continuing belief that this was to be Saints' year, told the *Echo* that, "delighted" as he was, "they've still got to be beaten. I expect that Palace will also be pleased to have avoided a First Division club."

The First Division camps were not only displeased but dismissive. Archie Gemmill felt that the winner of the Hillsborough semi-final – in which his Derby side faced United, who had won their replay – already had their ribbons on the Cup: "with all due respect," he says in his recent autobiography, neither of the other semi-finalists "were expected to trouble either Manchester United or us."

And Tommy Docherty famously remarked that this would be "the first-time a Cup Final will be played at Hillsborough. The other semi-final is a bit of a joke, really." The United manager can be forgiven for that witticism, in the light of the gracious way in which he would accept what the jokers eventually achieved – sentiments repeated in his generous foreword to this book.

Opposite: A cacophony of delight greets the draw.

Left to right: Channon, McCalliog, O'Brien (mostly hidden), Osgood, Stokes, Steele, Rodrigues, Blyth and Gilchrist, around a portable radio.
Two players are not part of the excitement: O'Brien has withdrawn, as befits a man about to be transferred, while Blyth has the I-told-you-so insouciance of the man who had predicted the draw.

Semi-final

Stamford Bridge   **3 April 1976**

CRYSTAL PALACE 0   SOUTHAMPTON 2

Gilchrist, Peach (Pen)

Att: 52,810   Referee: Pat Partridge

THE F.A. CUP
SEMI-FINAL
CRYSTAL PALACE
V
SOUTHAMPTON
STAMFORD BRIDGE,
LONDON

Kick-off 3 p.m.
Saturday, April 3rd, 1976.

Price 20p
Official Souvenir Programme

CRYSTAL PALACE

1 PAUL HAMMOND
2 PETER WALL
3 JIM CANNON
4 PHIL HOLDER
5 IAN EVANS (capt)
6 DEREK JEFFRIES
7 ALAN WHITTLE
8 NICK CHATTERTON
9 DAVID SWINDLEHURST
10 PETER TAYLOR
11 JEFFERY JOHNSON
12

MANAGER: MALCOLM ALLISON

SOUTHAMPTON

IAN TURNER 1
PETER RODRIGUES (capt) 2
DAVID PEACH 3
NICK HOLMES 4
MEL BLYTH 5
JIM STEELE 6
HUGH FISHER 7
MICK CHANNON 8
PETER OSGOOD 9
JIM McCALLIOG 10
BOBBY STOKES 11
PAUL GILCHRIST 12

MANAGER: LAWRIE McMENEMY

Team Changes

PALACE	5 Jeffries	6 Evans	7 Chatterton	8 Johnson
	9 Whittle	10 Swindlehurst 11 Taylor	12 Jump
SAINTS	7 Gilchrist	12 Fisher	

Highlights

Fisher declared self less than 100 % fit, so Gilchrist started.
A scrappy opening in a swirling gusty wind.
One first-half threat each: 40-yard shot from Jeffries went high;
Osgood shot blocked by Hammond.

40 mins: McCalliog booked for foul on Holder.
HT 0-0

60 mins: Osgood headed McCalliog's corner inches over; then booked
for tussle with Chatterton.
74 mins: 1-0 **Gilchrist** took pass from Osgood to shoot home from 25 yds.
79 mins: 2-0 Channon bundled over by Jeffries – possibly outside area. **Peach**
scored from pen.
85 mins: Channon dragged wide.
FT 2-0

45

The draw made, a venue had to be determined. Hillsborough and Villa Park had established a near-monopoly of semi-finals and, replays apart, the capital had staged only four semi-finals since the War, all of them in north London. Stamford Bridge had housed a replay the previous season but had not otherwise been selected for a semi-final since 1927.

Southampton had lost to Arsenal on that occasion. In fact, three of the club's five losing semi-finals to date had been at the Bridge. But, then, this was Palace's first-ever appearance in a semi-final. Not that such statistics were likely to worry the players. Ian Turner felt it "it didn't matter" to them where they played, "but we were happy for the fans that it was Stamford Bridge."

Peter Osgood and Jim McCalliog were more than happy at the choice of venue. Osgood was – and always will be – a Chelsea legend, while McCalliog had begun his professional career there. Ossie thought returning to the Bridge was quite simply "incredible". For Mel Blyth, it was a matter of playing against his former team-mates, with many of whom he was still friends. He'd got into the habit of dropping in for a cup of tea at their training ground in Mitcham, when he arrived back in London from a morning's training in Southampton: "I told one newspaper that they stopped me doing it, but they didn't really. It did get very tense, though."

Much of the media attention was on Third Division Palace, who were even being talked up, in some quarters, as favourites: Paul Bennett has "always thought that funny," but puts it down to "the Malcolm Allison effect." Indeed – the Palace manager had courted publicity throughout their Cup run, with his trademark fedora and, most famously, by inviting glamour model, Fiona Richmond, to join him and his players in the team-bath.

The Saints players weren't unduly bothered and in some ways probably benefited from the focus being elsewhere. David Peach reckons Allison "did us a favour by taking the pressure off us," while it was Jim McCalliog's turn to be wound up by the behaviour and predictions of their opponents.

> We prepared in the usual way but Malcolm Allison's carry-on motivated us. I remember talking to Terry Venables [the Palace coach] and he said they were going to beat us. It really got me going because I knew we had a better side. Apart from Peter Taylor, they had nobody to really worry about.

As the game approached, Saints' League form dipped alarmingly. Having lost consecutive away matches, at York and Luton, just before the Sixth Round, they had since lost at Fulham; drawn both at Chelsea and at home to Carlisle United; and then suffered a three-goal mauling at Sunderland, the eventual champions, on the Saturday before the semi-final.

Having remained in the side after the win at Bradford, Bennett feels that a defensive mix-up between him and Ian Turner – which resulted in the only goal at Craven Cottage – had ended his hopes of starting at Stamford Bridge.

I thought it was Ian's ball and that he should have cleared it. I knew then that I would be dropped so I wasn't too hopeful of playing in the semi-final. At the start of the week, it wasn't decided what the team would be, but it became clear I wouldn't be playing and I went to see Lawrie. He told me I wouldn't be involved, even as sub, which was hard – especially because Hughie was carrying an injury.

Hugh Fisher had enjoyed an unbroken run of games that went back to November, but that came to an end after the trip to Roker Park. He had been carrying an injury, deep in the stomach muscles, since January and it was now "getting pretty bad and just running was really painful."

Fisher wasn't the only player on the treatment table. Although Nick Holmes had recovered and played at Sunderland, Blyth had a calf-strain and Peter Rodrigues was nursing a heel injury. Each of them would start in the semi-final but Hughie wouldn't.

> Lawrie gave me every chance. Don Taylor worked with me and I had a serious fitness test on the Friday. They really pushed me and then Lawrie asked me for an honest answer. I felt that I wasn't 100 per cent fit. It was tempting to risk it, but I had lost a bit of mobility and it wouldn't have been fair to have said I could play just for the sake of being there. It would have been terrible to have played and in some way been responsible if we had lost.

In order to prepare for the game away from the growing clamour, whether for interviews or tickets, McMenemy took his team to Frinton-on-Sea on the Wednesday before the game. He explained why this would help: "there are no outside pressures, only the players eating and sleeping football together – all of them establishing a common aim."

The absence of pubs notwithstanding, the players do like to be beside the seaside.
Back row (*left to right*): Turner, Peach, Jim Clunie.
Front: Holmes, Gilchrist, Earles, Bennett, Osgood, Fisher, Channon, Steele.

If avoiding "outside pressures" was a key objective, he also knew that there were no pubs or clubs in Frinton. What he hadn't bargained for was a private function that three of his players chanced upon. And it might have come as something of a surprise to him that his trusted captain was involved.

> Lawrie was strict and we knew the line and didn't try and cross it but the two Jims [Steele and McCalliog] invited me out for a stroll and we happened upon a bar where there was a private party going on. I remember standing with one of the guests, doing a six-foot crossword and drinking half a lager from a jam jar. We didn't get drunk, but we did get back about 45 minutes after curfew. As we came in, I could hear Lawrie talking to the coaches. We scampered off to our rooms and thought we had got away with it. The next morning, Lawrie named the three of us in front of everyone and said "if we lose on Saturday, I will blame you three." My head just dropped – as did the other two. Ted Bates made a remark and broke the spell, but I felt pretty bad.

David Peach applauds the way the manager generally allowed his players room to breathe: "Lawrie was great. We played a bit of golf to relax and a couple of the lads went to the races." During one of the training sessions at Frinton, Mel Blyth took it upon himself to brief his team-mates about his old club.

> Lawrie didn't ask me to, but I went through their entire team with our lads. Peter Taylor was carrying a knock, which I knew, so I told Pedro to give him a hard tackle early on. I spoke to Taylor after the game and he was a pal, but we did what we had to do. I told Ossie and Mick that, if we played our "A" game and they played theirs, we would beat them.

***

On the march... getting tickets

How to get tickets for Stamford Bridge? The obvious move was to find a season-ticket holder at that ground, whose entitlement I could exploit. That had worked at Villa Park in 1963 and would again at Highbury in 1984. The trouble was that I knew no Chelsea fans.

Fortunately, my old school-friend and Saints fan, Ian, did. Problem solved. He queued and got four tickets. Dad and Malcolm, a Saints-supporting Bristol friend, joined us on the day.
David Bull

I was – and still am – living in West London so, when Chelsea, as the host club, put their allocation on general sale on a Sunday morning, off I went at 6.00 am, ready to queue for four hours. By happy chance, Crystal Palace were selling tickets at Selhurst Park that day, but when I arrived at Stamford Bridge, in the dark, I found a red-and-white queue snaking round. A happy four-hour Saints party then took place – we got our tickets and, by another happy chance, they were in the Shed end where, a week or so later, I joined the rest of the standing Saints fans.
Andrew Wrigley

Back in Southampton, club secretary Keith Honey was dealing with the unprecedented demand for tickets. After season-ticket and voucher-holders had been given a fortnight to claim a ticket, general sale on the Tuesday before the match saw 5,500 tickets sold in less than four hours. Realising that demand had seriously outweighed supply, Honey then approached Chelsea to see whether they had any unsold tickets from their allocation as host club. This produced a further 500, which were sold the next morning in just 50 minutes. It meant that Saints would have 21,500 supporters at the game.

The journey to the ground on match day had elements of a *Carry On* film. David Peach explains.

> On the way to the ground, we found ourselves alongside the Palace bus. Lawrie told our driver to get in front of them, which he did and which we all enjoyed. It meant they were behind us as we drove into the Stamford Bridge car park.

Once they were off the bus, and before settling in to the dressing room to change and prepare, as was the custom in those days, the players walked out onto the pitch at around 1.45 pm. Normally, only the keenest fans would witness this ritual but, on this occasion, Peach was aware that "for a change, the ground was nearly full, even then."

Mel Blyth was doing everything possible to block out of his mind the fact that his wife's pregnancy had nearly run its full term. He had arranged for a friend to be with her at the match, which she insisted on watching, with a number to call if the birth started. Both teams went out on the pitch at the same time, when Malcolm Allison not only helped Blyth, inadvertently, to focus on non-domestic matters but also put his fedora at risk: "he was putting up his fingers to indicate 2-0 to the Palace fans. I told him there was no way that they would beat us and we had a bet. I bet him his fedora against £50."

As expected, Jim Steele was in his regular slot alongside Blyth, while Fisher's honesty about his lingering injury meant Paul Gilchrist starting on the right of midfield, with Nick Holmes back on the left. Holmes

Allison was willing to put his hat – even his fedora – on a Palace win.

recalls McMenemy's team-talk. It would seem that, by this stage of the build-up, Allison's posturing, assisted by Venables, had stirred up several of Lawrie's players, but there was still scope for him to counter his opponent's showmanship with what the statistics showed.

He went through everyone in our team and listed the number of appearances that we'd had. Then he did the same for Palace. Ours came to thousands, where theirs came to hundreds. He then said that was it: we were better and more experienced. Apart from me, everyone in the team had made hundreds of appearances. He would use the same technique for the Final.

There was, however, the matter of Peter Taylor. Despite playing in the Third Division, the Palace winger had made his England debut the week before, coming on as a substitute for Channon and scoring against Wales at Wrexham. Rodrigues recalls McMenemy's emphasis on the likely threat from Taylor and how they would have to keep an eye on him. In the event, the Saints skipper tackled him very early in the game and effectively ended the threat he posed.

Rodrigues insists that he was not following Blyth's advice to give his opponent an early knock: "I caught his knee but it was a pure accident. I was clearing the ball but I followed through and caught him. I would never try and hurt a fellow pro deliberately and I don't ever think about it now because it was an accident." Taylor has never doubted that: "I don't think, and I never did, that Peter set out to injure me. It was just a tackle that I didn't see coming, but it definitely affected my performance. I felt about 80 per cent for the rest of the game."

Both the goals came in the second half, with Saints attacking the famous Shed end where their fans were standing. Gilchrist got the breakthrough-goal after a one-two with Osgood.

> The goal was one of those things that wasn't planned in any way. I played the one-two and because no one challenged I just decided to have a shot. I think their 'keeper was probably unsighted and I remember seeing the net move, hearing the crowd and then realising it had gone in. Of course, had Hughie been fully fit, he probably would have played but that is just the way things go. He was so honest to say he wasn't 100 per cent fit.

As the Saints fans celebrate, the shot from Gilchrist (out of picture) is followed in by Osgood (No. 9), Blyth (No. 5) and Channon (No. 8) – who claims the ball brushed his leg.

Mick Channon has always argued, somewhat mischievously, that he could have claimed that goal. "Gillie's shot did touch my sock and in theory it was another goal I should have had, but I wouldn't take it away from him – but I definitely got the last touch."

Five minutes later, Channon's influence was not open to debate as he won a penalty when brought down by Jeffries. Channon had been the penalty-taker but had missed a fortnight before. David Peach stepped up to the plate. Southampton fans would later come to expect Peach to score regularly from the spot – if not quite at the inimitable success-rate of Matt Le Tissier. But this was his first for the Saints, so the fans didn't know what to expect. Nor, it seems, did Peach.

> My old arse was twitching. Normally a pen was fine but I realised, all of a sudden, from Gillingham in the Fourth Division… if I score I'm going to Wembley. I shouldn't have thought like that and it wasn't my best penalty. Normally, I picked a side and placed it and, even if the goalkeeper stood on that side, I wouldn't change my mind. This time, I just smashed it. Luckily, Hammond went the wrong way because, if he had just stood up, he would have stopped it.
>
> As it went in, I ran to the side of the pitch to look for my mum and dad but, before I could look up, I was mobbed. We knew we were there then.

As Hammond dives to his left, Peach "smashes" his spot-kick straight down the middle.

The players all agree that they had been confident, but not cock-sure, going into the game. As Ian Turner describes it, they also took on board the words of Osgood, Rodrigues and McCalliog, who had all played in FA Cup Finals: "no-one remembers the two teams that don't win through to the Final."

At the final whistle, a tremendous celebration started and the players were quick to share their joy with the supporters. Peter Rodrigues had a small matter to resolve with the manager, but his first thoughts were for the fans.

It's hugs all-round from Mel Blyth
at the final whistle.

Above: Having won a fedora,
he commiserates with Wall,
his former team-mate.

Below: He and his manager
sandwich Rodrigues.

The supporters had been good throughout the Cup run and they were spot-on that day. You draw from the fans when you score, or if you are struggling and need a lift. Once we had won, it was total elation, which we shared with them. Then I gave Lawrie a hug and said "what was the problem?" I knew I had stepped over the mark in Frinton. It was out of character for me but, in later life, when I got into the licensed trade, I always put it down to Osgood, Steele and McCalliog who, when I first came to Saints, made it their business to take me to every pub in town. I reckon I always bought the drinks but I didn't mind: they were great lads.

Hugh Fisher remained on the bench for the whole match and accepts that the manager's decision to give him a role was probably out of kindness.

I think some people would say for a manager to have sentiment is a weakness, but I am almost certain he did it on sentiment alone so that I should be part of it, even though I was probably only 90 per cent fit.

It didn't feel good to be sitting on the side. It was very disappointing and, like most players would be, I didn't feel part of it – although, looking back, I actually was. The euphoria when we won helped me to push my personal disappointment aside and look at the bigger picture: Gillie had come in and scored that brilliant goal and the rest is history.

Bennett similarly overcame his disappointment: the semi-final was a "brilliant" experience, in which "those who didn't play were kept involved." Indeed, it was very much a club event: as the champagne flowed in the dressing-room afterwards, Peach was delighted, he recalls, that it was such "a great day for Ted Bates and George Reader," Chief Executive and Chairman, respectively. Yet Channon found it "a bit of an anti-climax."

In the back of my mind was the thought that no-one remembers who comes second, not in the Derby or in any Cup Final, so I was thinking it was all very well getting there: now we had to win the bloody thing.

Meanwhile, there was the small matter of the Blyth/Allison wager to be resolved. Mel remembers the door opening and the hat being thrown in. The following week, Nigel Clarke of the *Daily Mirror* arranged for a picture to be taken at Blyth's home and then, on 14 April, his daughter Kelly was born.

The team left the ground on the bus and, according to McCalliog, "Ossie got Lawrie to stop for a drink and we went into a pub full of Saints fans. It was absolutely brilliant. We stayed for about an hour. Then we got back to Southampton and it was even better." Bennett likewise enjoyed the "marvellous trip home. We had stopped at the *Winning Post* in Richmond and then, when we got back to Southampton, we went to the *After Eight* club in Shirley. I don't think I have ever been as drunk in my life." Meanwhile, Blyth headed back home to Sanderstead.

As I left the ground, there were loads of Palace fans waiting. I had put two fingers up at the end, meaning we won 2-0, but as we went through the gates to the car, one of them asked me how I could do it. I thought she meant beating them, but she meant sticking two fingers up. I would never have done that – I had too many friends and a great following there – but I had to remonstrate with them.

Afterwards, they never collected my dustbins for about three months. I got some stick with graffiti on my walls. It said YOU USED TO BE A CRYSTAL PALACE FAVOURITE, BUT NOW… I got slated.

The truth was, though, that it had been men against boys.

From the other side…

Mick Channon stayed at my house after the England game, the week before the semi-final. He "arse-slipped" down the stairs and he could have been injured. If he had missed the game because of an accident at my house, it would have looked as though it was deliberate.

I didn't feel any extra weight of responsibility about being viewed as Palace's star. I was just a confident young man playing well. If I was playing today, I would be more aware; but I was just enjoying my football. I think both teams could have played a lot better. My memory of the day is that it should have finished 0-0 and then both teams could have played a lot better in a replay. In the end, Southampton took their chances and we didn't. Just before Gilchrist scored, we had a very good chance, with Ian Evans about five yards out from a corner. It was tense affair from two teams desperate to get to the Final.

We had had Malcolm Allison's high profile all through the Cup run and obviously had won every match up to that point, so it would be unfair to say it was a hindrance. I remember Peter Osgood was wound up by it, but I don't think it affected us. The most pleasing thing for us, as players, was playing in London where our fans could see us, because all the previous rounds seemed to be up north: Sunderland, Leeds, Scarborough. And remember we had started in the First Round, so it had been a long road.

I watched the Final and I was pleased for Southampton.

Peter Taylor

On the march: Superstars hooligan...

Mick Channon gave me his bib from *Superstars* **[the BBC 1 series in which Channon was a favourite] when I was over at his stables in Bishops Waltham, helping to get some footings in. He was a big friend of mine, by then.**

I wore it to Stamford Bridge – with my red-and-white sombrero. It was the Year of the Hat: I thought I'd out-do Allison's fedora. I had a Stand ticket from Mick. I was so excited at the end, but I can't understand how I was able to come straight down through the Stand and on to the pitch. Nobody stopped me. I got right out to the middle, somehow, and lifted Mick up.

He tells everybody I was "the first football hooligan".
George Tomkins

As the cameramen waylay Holmes (*left*) and Fisher,
George Tomkins has got on to the pitch to thank Channon for his ticket.

On the march: remember the day…

This game was, for me, just as memorable as the Final itself – if not more so.

Having grown up in London, I was returning to a ground that my dad had taken me to many times. So I was sad that he had given up his ticket to one of my mates – nine of us travelled up in a minibus from Gosport. Dad would make sure to use it for the Final, though.

David Weaver.

I sat in the front row of the main stand, my usual calm self, kicking every ball and questioning whether the referee had a birth certificate. But I became aware of the chap sitting to the left of me: whatever happened on the field, he just sat there impassively.

So, at half-time, I asked him who he was supporting. "No-one, really," he said, "but I will win £2,000 if Crystal Palace beat Southampton." When Paul Gilchrist scored, Mr Left still sat there, showing no emotion whatsoever. Of course, when Dave Peach scored, the place took off. Total strangers were hugging each other; I even embraced my wife.

When I eventually sat down, Mr Left had left, stage left.

Don't you just hate bad losers?

Jim Dolbear

Before the game, we were talking to some Palace supporters, who really thought they were going to win. I must admit I was very nervous: I'd rather lose in the Final than the semis.

Two minutes before the kick-off, a "man mountain" came and stood right in front of me, so that I couldn't see the pitch. He turned round and asked "can you see?" "No", so we swapped places. If he hadn't asked, I wouldn't have said anything: he was a big bloke.

When we scored the first goal, I remember being grasped in a bear-hug and being raised off my feet. When I got back down to earth, I turned round and it was him. "Sorry," he said: "got carried away". Same thing happened for the second goal, but at least I was prepared.

When the final whistle went, I turned to shake his hand and celebrate, but he was just stood there. He had tears running down his face. Tears of joy. I shook his hand. I'd never seen a grown man cry before, let alone at a football match.

Dave Webster

On the march — and on the telly...

Even before the kick-off, the Shed end was a mass of red and a riot of noise. The Palace end seemed subdued by comparison.

The match was awful but, when the final whistle went, then, perhaps for the first time, the fans embraced Lawrie McMenemy. Amid the amazing scenes of excitement and ecstasy, I kissed my friend Andy's mum, telling her how wonderful it was that "an elderly lady" like her was present: she would have been in her early forties. We went back to the car, passing disconsolate Palace fans, still wearing their fedoras.

When we got home, we watched the Brotherhood of Man win the Eurovision Song Contest with *Save Your Kisses For Me*. It was followed by *Match of the Day*, featuring Manchester United's 2-0 win over Derby County. In the post-match interviews, United's two-goal hero, Gordon Hill, was in a buoyant mood. When questioned on the prospect of playing Southampton in the Final, he mockingly asked "Southampton, Southampton, who are they?" He would soon find out.

Steve Eckersley

In other news...

The country's new Prime Minister was Hampshire-born James Callaghan. A former Chancellor of the Exchequer and Home Secretary, he had beaten Employment Secretary Michael Foot by 176 votes to 137.

The press had already dubbed the new PM "Sailor Jim", in recognition of his war-time service as an ordinary seaman. It was a remarkable turn-around for a politician who had resigned as Chancellor after he was forced to devalue the pound in 1967.

His time in office was to be fraught with difficulty as a result of his government losing its slim majority. He would be forced to make deals with the minority parties including the alliance with the Liberals in 1977, known as the Lib-Lab Pact. The power cuts and strikes in the "Winter of Discontent" would follow in 1978 and eventually, in March 1979, he would be forced to call a general election that would usher in Margaret Thatcher's government.

The weekend's big television movie was *The Guns Of Navarone*, starring David Niven, Gregory Peck and Anthony Quinn, on ITV, and the *TV Times* trumpeted the return of Elsie Tanner to *Coronation Street*.

Noel Edmonds kicked off the year's Radio 1 Roadshows and Simon Bates was the new Sunday morning presenter.

Britain's Eurovision winner, Brotherhood of Man's *Save Your Kisses For Me*, was Number 1 on the charts.

Now for the Final

Interviewed after the Final, Lawrie McMenemy would explain to Jimmy Hill that he had "expected" his players "to be less than choirboys at times" – that went with having "a lot of ability and a lot of flair."

But after he had dealt successfully with the curfew-violation at Frinton in the build-up to the semi-final, his patience must have been tried by the prolonged revelries that followed their win, especially since two of the Frinton Three – Jim McCalliog and Jim Steele – were again involved, this time with Peter Osgood.

McCalliog is most reticent on the matter, saying only that "the boss handled us as he always did. OK, we got fined but that was it with no real fuss afterwards." That may be so, but there was plenty of fuss at the time. After a Sunday off, when the players could celebrate as they wished, it was business as usual on the Monday morning: training in preparation for the local derby at Fratton Park the following evening. Osgood was more forthcoming than McCalliog: "The boss told us to make our own way to Hayling Island, where we were staying that night. In the background, the 'moos' started, because that meant we were going to *The Cowherds*," the pub at the other end of Northlands Road from The Dell.

While the majority of the squad followed orders, the threesome who got a little carried away arrived 15 minutes after the 11 pm curfew. Steele was first to get there.

> I was met by George Horsfall who said "Lawrie says you can just go home." I sat on the steps and waited for the other two and then told them to hold the taxi. We went to Pompey and found a nightclub. It made the headlines, the next morning: *Star three might not play in Final* – that kind of thing. We knew that couldn't happen, but it was a bit dodgy at the time.

Steve Williams, Paul Bennett and Pat Earles were the main beneficiaries of McMenemy's anger. Having made his debut as sub in the Third Round, Earles had come off the bench in the last two League games. But this would be his first start and Williams's first appearance of any kind. For Bennett, it was a last chance to stake a claim to play at Wembley.

With both Jim Clunie and George Horsfall on duty in Hayling Island, it was left to Bill Ellerington – the former coach who had become Chief Scout two seasons earlier – to marshall the reinforcements on the Tuesday morning. Bennett recalls how Ellerington "got hold of me, Pat and Stevie and told us to get down to Portsmouth. I asked why and he said 'Never mind: just get down there.' When I got there, I found out I was playing and why."

Earles seems to have had a moment of prescience that morning: "I dropped my wife off at work and said 'wouldn't it be great to get the call to say I was playing?' And that was exactly what happened. What a game to make a debut – there were police dogs out and everything."

His wife, Sandra, had sufficient notice to get there and watch Saints win, Channon scoring the only goal in the final minute. This result virtually sealed the fate of Pompey, who had been occupying a relegation spot all season. If that pleased those Southampton fans who preferred their neighbours to be relegated rather than have local derbies, the more immediate question of interest, surely, was what would happen to the curfew-breakers, especially the two recidivists.

All three of their replacements had acquitted themselves well, but there was never a doubt in Osgood's mind that normality would be restored before it came to the Cup Final: "I wasn't worried about my place. We had stepped out of line and were correctly punished, but I knew we would get back in." Steele, who had good reason to be familiar with the manager's disciplinary methods, blames McMenemy, slightly tongue-in-cheek, for allowing them to make their own way.

> He used to do these things like that. We'd go up to the Sports Centre and do these two-mile runs. Then he'd tell us to make our own way back to The Dell. So, one time, Ossie and I got the bus and started waving to the lads going down Hill Lane. He fined us £40 each but we said "you told us to make our own way back." I'm sure a lawyer would have got us off, but we still got fined.

About two weeks before the Final, Steele was called in by McMenemy, who had been getting reports that Jim had been seen in a pub on a Friday night. Steele assured him that he "hadn't been drinking at all, but he was still concerned that I had been in a pub." Jim had to explain that he "lived in the pub, literally, because I lived above the *Drummond Arms* in Portswood, which was run by ex-Saint, Jimmy McGowan. Lawrie just put his head in his hands and said 'Oh no!' I told him I got bored on a Friday night, so I went down to the bar for company."

Once the furore of the extended celebrations had died down, the preparations for the Final began in earnest. If ever the term "Cup Fever" was warranted to describe the mood of a city, it was in Southampton through April 1976. Countless conversations must have started with "have you got a ticket?" and the different means by which those tickets were obtained were also countless, too (see just a few examples, *below and opposite*).

On the march... getting tickets

I was on a kibbutz near Haifa in Israel. Through the BBC World Service and *Jerusalem Post*, I had kept abreast of Saints' Cup run and even managed to catch a TV News-clip of Mike Channon scoring in the West Brom replay.

As soon as the semi-final result came through, it was time to airmail friends and relatives, imploring them to get me a ticket, and to book my flight home. I arrived back to good news – a ticket had been obtained for £25: 10 times face-value – and bad news: it was for the Man U end. One of the tensest moments of my life was swapping tickets with a United fan outside Wembley, so we could both be at the "right" end. I could so easily have ended up with no ticket and a sore head. But all went well and I was in.

Richard Atkinson

While my wife Kate and I had queued at The Dell for our two semi-final tickets, my membership of the London Saints Supporters Club enabled me to get only one for the Final.

But I saw a tiny advert in the "Classifieds" of the *London Evening Standard*, offering tickets for "every occasion". When I rang the advertised number, I was directed to an address in East London. I went by Underground and came eventually to a tumbledown third-floor council flat in a very dodgy area. I knocked on the door, which was opened just a crack to see who I was and why I had called. I was then ushered into a room that was totally empty apart from a large wardrobe which, when opened, revealed thousands of tickets for every event under the sun. I paid my £40 for the ticket (face-value £2.50) and left very hurriedly.

I was glad to get back on the train, where I took my first proper look at the ticket. Stamped on the back was

THE DELL, MILTON ROAD, SOUTHAMPTON.

Thank goodness! But I still wonder how my ticket had got to a ticket tout: from which player's allocation had it reached East London?

Peter Horne

THE DELL, MILTON ROAD, SOUTHAMPTON. PLAN OF STADIUM TURNSTILES

This ticket is issued subject to the Rules and Regulations of Wembley Stadium Limited and upon the express conditions that the holder thereof shall not take a Camera or photographic apparatus or recording apparatus of any description into the Stadium, nor shall the holder take any cinematograph picture or photograph or recording of any kind. The possession of this ticket shall constitute an acceptance by the holder of the above conditions and imply an undertaking on his (or her) part to observe the same and also an admission of the right of Wembley Stadium Limited to confiscate any camera and/or photographic or recording apparatus, film or plates or tapes in the holder's possession; further, the holder of this ticket is requested not to stand in any gangway or in any stairway and to obey the instructions of the officials in this connection. No money refunded or tickets exchanged. Admission is at ticket holder's own risk.
THIS TICKET IS ISSUED ON THE CONDITION THAT IT IS NOT RE-SOLD FOR MORE THAN ITS FACE VALUE.

While pleased with myself when it came to getting semi-final tickets (in a tried-and-trusted way described earlier), I didn't know where to begin with tickets for Wembley. I'd not then read the Cyril Smith story (overleaf), but rather assumed MPs received an allocation. So I rang one, whom I knew not to be into football. Yes, he'd had a ticket, but had passed it on to a constituent. Never mind: the father of a Lancaster friend knew Tom Finney. Turned out he didn't know him that well, though. But then Malcolm, who'd had one of my semi-final tickets, struck gold. His fiancée's dad knew a Plymouth Argyle director. So two tickets for Malcolm and me. Sometime later, at their wedding, I was told the said director was there and "don't mention the tickets!" Malcolm was supposed to have taken his bride-to-be to Wembley, not me.

David Bull

I remember my mate Graham ringing, when I had given up on a ticket, saying that he had two tickets from his cousin: he was the postman to The Dell and had been given them to ensure he wasn't tempted by all the Cup Final mail going in and out. Can that really be true?

Andrew Wrigley

At the time, the *Echo* reported the quite remarkable tactics employed by 11 year-old Glenn Wheeler-Osman and his friend, 12 year-old George Fabling. They were pupils at Applemore School in Dibden where the headmaster, Alan Dove, was a friend of Cyril Smith, the Liberal MP for Rochdale. Smith was famous as a larger-than-life character, who was also a lot larger than the average man. He was a passionate Rochdale fan and, when he visited the school, he told the first-year reading class that all the best football teams were from the North. The two boys argued that Saints were best, prompting Smith to promise that, if Southampton reached the Cup Final, he would get them two tickets.

So, after the semi-final, Glenn wrote to the House of Commons and reminded the MP of his promise. Two days before the game, Smith rang to invite them both to Westminster, where he produced two £6 Cup Final seats, obtained from his Liberal colleagues, Stephen Ross, MP for the Isle of Wight, and Jo Grimond, the party's former leader.

Meanwhile, the *Echo* had been reporting sightings of fans arriving from the USA and the far corners of the Commonwealth. Thus we learned that Hubert Barter had come from Florida; Geoff Winteridge from Freemantle, Australia; and Terry Prowse from Toronto.

Terry Prowse, home from Toronto, shows off his hat – and the natty attire of his niece, Zoe – to an *Echo* photographer, watched by his parents, Irene and Alfred.

Ray Terris was not met by the cameras over here, but he did get himself snapped as he was about to leave Australia for the flight home.

For the majority of Saints fans, the message was clear: turn up in the right week with the right piece of paper and buy your ticket: £2.50 standing; £5 to £10 for a seat. There would be no postal sales, Club Secretary, Keith Honey, told the *Echo*: "the danger of valuable tickets going astray is too great. I hope everyone will cooperate for this historic occasion."

It wasn't quite as simple as that – as you can see from the queue-stories *opposite* – with the office under pressure from the Monday after the semi-final. Honey told the *Echo*, the next day, that he had already received enquiries from Saints fans – or so they claimed – in China and Uganda and had had "a lot of applications from Manchester United supporters," who weren't pretending otherwise, it seems.

Season ticket-holders, commencing Sunday 11 April, for a week: When I arrived that Sunday afternoon, there were two queues: one for the Stand that housed the Royal Box; the other for the Stand opposite. Me, I just wanted a terrace ticket and, although there was no such queue, that was what I'd ask for.

To be honest, there wasn't enough info the way you would get it today, via a steward's megaphone, as to which queue was supposed to be what. But that didn't excuse the fuss being made over those poor souls who had perhaps gone into the wrong line: you'd have thought that getting a ticket near the Royal Box was a matter of life-and-death. I sensed the presence of "latch-on" supporters and, sure enough, the argument was, suddenly, all about who was a true fan or not – "show us your medals!" – and I confess to stirring it: "didn't see you at Villa Park in '63 – or the promotion run-in of '66," etc.

When I finally got to the front of the queue and asked for a ticket behind the goal, the clerk paused, then went back to dig out my ticket from a separate drawer. It was quite clear from his reaction that he hadn't had to do that so far. I may well, then, have been the *very first* Saints fan to purchase a *terrace* ticket for the 1976 FA Cup Final.

Chris Newman

Voucher-holders, Sunday 18 April, for a week: We panicked and went down Saturday tea-time with our blankets. We joined a queue of similarly-minded fans in Milton Road. I remember playing football in the road during the night and a lad in the queue kept us entertained with his hilarious impressions, especially of Frank Spencer. There was a good atmosphere, in general, but we were told that a coach-load of Man U fans – apparently coming down for tickets – had been stopped, and turned back, at Winchester. Some time that Sunday morning, we got our tickets.

Phil Rawlings

General sales, Monday 26 April: A holder of neither a season-ticket nor a voucher – I was away at university – I'd come home to queue with my Uncle Eric. Although a Hammer, he had inducted me as a Saint in August 1966.

When I joined the queue at about 3.00 am on the Sunday, it stretched around the back of the Milton Road end and was very good-natured. People were sharing food, drinks and newspapers but, as more fans arrived, the tension rose – particularly if it was felt anyone was trying to push in. But then they opened the ticket office, a day early, and there was a new anxiety, as rumours spread back along the queue that there were only 100… 50… NO tickets left. And so on… yet now I was at the ticket-window, producing my semi-final ticket and giving my name and address, to prove that I wasn't one of those Man U fans, rumoured to have come down to get some of our tickets. Hand over our £2.50 each… tickets in hand… we were going.

Nigel Hale

He took that early opportunity to assure fans that the priorities used for the semi-final – season tickets; vouchers; general sales – would again be followed

Vouchers had been issued on 31 January, when Oldham Athletic and a total of 14,294 fans came to The Dell. That was a bold move by the club as the Saints had just been drawn away to West Brom. By the same token, you needed to be an optimist to keep your voucher safe: there is perhaps another book to be written on the experiences of those who had a voucher but couldn't quite remember where they'd put it.

All in all, the ticket-sales operation severely tested the club's meagre resources – even after Honey had borrowed from within.

> Guy Askham was financial director of the club and he lent us the services of one of his senior clerks to look after the financial side of selling the tickets. I had one young lad, Denys Raynor, as assistant secretary; Barbara Oakshott was my secretary; Peggy Worlock was office clerk; and we had a part-time clerk called Madge. That was it for staff.

In fact, Peggy had left the club a few months before to work at Southampton General Hospital, but she answered the call to come back and help out. Not that she felt she had an option: her husband, Monty, "was Ted Bates's best friend. Ted had been best man at our wedding and I am godmother to Jo Bates [Ted and Mary's daughter], so I could hardly refuse the request to help out." Honey and she agree that the voucher system worked well and that most, if not all, of the fans who deserved to get a ticket were successful, although Honey was obliged "to go ex-directory because we were getting 'phone calls at midnight from people asking for tickets."

It was the police who rang him shortly before midnight on the Saturday before the Final. Tickets were due to go on general sale come Monday morning, but fans had begun queuing on Saturday afternoon before the game with Hull City. They were joined by some of those who had decided to watch the match first and, by 9.30 pm, the police were asking for the floodlights to be switched on in the Dell carpark. By 11pm, the queue was so long that the police rang Honey and asked him to start selling a day early.

His staff duly opened for business at 9.00 am on Sunday and had sold out by 2.30 pm, with the queue still stretching out of the carpark, along the Milton Road end of the ground and beyond. Despite announcements by the club on local and national radio, the news of the Sunday opening and sell-out seems not to have reached those who began to form a new queue at 4.15 am on Monday. When they refused to accept that the tickets were all gone, the police again woke the Secretary for confirmation. The queue continued to grow, however, and it required a further statement, this time from Honey over the loudspeaker, before the crowd dispersed.

The disappointment would have been considerably more widespread if Manchester United had had their way: their average League gate for the season was over 54,000, compared with Southampton's of under 17,000, so they

The disappointed fans, who had refused to believe the POLICE NOTICE, disperse after a loud-speaker announcement by the Club Secretary.

reasoned that they should have a greater share of the tickets. Honey had to put the case for equality against proportionality: "The FA backed us but my opposite number in Manchester, Les Olive, was not a happy man."

Honey was "pleased", overall, with the way his team handled the sales operation, but admits it was "pretty stressful: we were in unknown territory." It was certainly a big change for the man who had joined the club from Exeter City in 1966 and who would stay for 13 years.

Lawrie McMenemy was doing his best to keep the players focussed on the job in hand, but the clamour for tickets inevitably intruded on their preparations. In Jim McCalliog's case, a simple act of kindness caused a situation to develop that could have had serious consequences. He had given a pair of tickets to his sister, who worked in a travel agency. She offered them as a prize in a customer-promotion and, after a national newspaper ran the story, the FA became involved. The manager's famous skills as a diplomat saved the day, but it was a lesson to all the squad members in how to handle their distribution of tickets.

Meanwhile, Ted Bates and Bill Ellerington were kept busy watching Manchester United. Ellerington had been with the club since 1940, famously vying with Alf Ramsey in 1948-49 for the right-back position – not only for Southampton but for England, too. He had always enjoyed scouting before switching to that role, full-time, and tends to get the credit for spotting Mick Channon (but see his denial at page 79). Now Bates and he had a four-week mission, during which they "watched United so much we knew what they had for breakfast. We were mainly concerned with how they would play as a team."

Actually, they had five games in which to watch United, while the Southampton players had seven matches in which to avoid getting injured.

As Ian Turner puts it, "you dreaded getting hurt. Our last game of the season was against Hull City and then, having got through that, you could relax a little because, barring a training-ground accident, you knew you were there."

But three of the side had come away from Stamford Bridge with worrying disciplinary records: they were approaching the 20-point mark, at which they would face an FA hearing and possible suspension. McCalliog was on 16 points, plus however many would be added for his semi-final booking; Steele was on 17, while Peach was precariously poised on 19 points.

The possibility of resting Peach was mooted, but he assured the manager that he was quite happy to carry on and keep out of trouble. McMenemy had other ideas, however. It was decided that Peach should get himself booked – in the way that David Beckham famously would, nearly 30 years later. If he could achieve this in the next match, then the timing of his disciplinary hearing and subsequent one-match suspension would be such that he missed the last League game against Hull, but would be available for the Final.

So it was that, at Fratton Park the following Tuesday, Peach contrived to reach the 20-mark. When a free-kick was given to Pompey, he repeatedly broke from the defensive wall, until the referee eventually booked him and, somewhat to the bemusement of the opposition, he was congratulated by his team-mates.

McMenemy went with Peach to the FA hearing but, while the manager was his usual, relaxed self, the player was more than a little concerned that the inevitable ban might be for *two* games and so preclude his appearance in the Cup Final.

To this day, he is baffled as to why the FA clerk, when reading his disciplinary record to the tribunal, made him out to be an exemplary footballer with a first-class conduct record: he is sure he had incurred many more bookings than was stated. Whatever the reason, it worked.

> I was called in and I got slaughtered. They dressed me down like a naughty schoolboy. Then Lawrie went in and told me not to worry, but I was worried. I got called back in after 45 minutes and the Chairman slaughtered me again and then said "we have had a long chat about this and our decision is to suspend you for one match starting from today. Have a good game in the Final."

A very relieved Peach was suspended for the Hull City game, at which he was presented with the supporters' *Player of the Year* award. The squad then went to the Selsdon Park Hotel to prepare. On the Thursday evening, they all sat down to dinner but, as per the manager's instructions, there was to be no alcohol. Peter Rodrigues describes the way they attempted to get round that rule.

> We were ordering things like melon with port, steak in red wine sauce and sherry trifle. After the meal, Lawrie was going to do a TV interview and he told Jim Clunie to let us have a lager before bed. Steelie asked Jim if we could have another half and he said "yes". I think, in a strange way, that helped us win the Cup because, if Jim had said "no", some of them might have gone looking for a drink

More than 80 of Paul Gilchrist's neighbours in Petworth Gardens, Lordswood, had signed a huge good-luck card for his send-off to Selsdon Park. Then some of them dressed up for the presentation by young Mark Knowles.

A symbolic moment – as the coach leaves to take the players to Selsdon Park, in preparation for the most significant day in the club's history, a romantic monument in that history is being pulled down: you can see, in the background, that the house in Archers Road – in which the manager and assistant secretary, Ted and Mary Bates, had lived over the laundry – is being demolished.

outside but, as it was, we then went to bed happy that we had been treated as responsible adults. The psychology of the approach from management was dead right and set us up on Final day.

David Peach, the fans' Player of the Year, in training at Selsdon Park Hotel.
As George Horsfall time-keeps, Steele (*right*) and Osgood wait their turn.

Jim McCalliog has a slightly different memory of that evening's psychology.

> Lawrie said we could have a quiet drink at the bar in the hotel, but we had to be in bed by 11pm. There was only me, Jim Steele and Jim Clunie left. JC looked nervous, puffing away on his cigarette and watching the clock, so I asked him what was up: did he have a big game on Saturday or something? He told me not to be so damn cocky. We waited until a minute to eleven, then went off to bed, laughing to ourselves.

On the Friday morning, a trip to Wembley was arranged for those who wished to go. Nick Holmes declined – he was happy to wait for Cup Final day – but most of the squad did go. As they were walking off the pitch, the Man Utd players arrived. McCalliog's "big mate" from the United side, Stuart "Pancho" Pearson, was there and so, too, was coach Tommy Cavanagh. Before leaving Old Trafford, Jim "had fallen out with Tommy, although I respected him."

> He came over to shake hands and said I should have been playing for them. I told him he'd got it wrong and that I didn't want to play for them. He asked me what I meant and I told him "we're going to beat you tomorrow." I looked him straight in the eye and Pancho was killing himself laughing. Cav got really angry and called me a so-and-so playboy. He was ranting and raving at me and Pancho was rolling about laughing.

Although most of the team were assured of their place – by this stage, Bennett knew he would not be playing – the question of Hugh Fisher's fitness was not resolved until the Friday. He had been working with Don Taylor all week but both men knew, with 24 hours to go, that he wouldn't make it. As he had before the semi-final, Fisher put the good of the team first and, with 30 years' perspective, is able to be philosophical about it.

> There are better players than me who have missed Cup Finals and it was great to be part of it. Lawrie gave me every chance but I knew, on the Friday, I wouldn't play in the Final. It never affected my relationship with Gillie and we are still good friends to this day. If I am honest, he probably brought slightly more of a goal-scoring threat to the team than I did, as he proved in the semi-final.

Gilchrist was ready and still carrying Mick Channon's post-semi-final comments in his head.

> He was exactly right about needing to win rather than just turn up. We didn't want to spend the rest of our lives regretting not performing in the Final. To get something that every footballer wants to do and then lose, well, you would regret that for the rest of your life.
>
> My place was never certain and nothing was said about who would play. They even printed programmes with me as substitute, but then Lawrie told me I was in. I hadn't been playing badly so I was happy to be in the side.

For Mel Blyth, it seemed everything was falling into place.

> Now the dream was becoming real. I had a beautiful baby daughter. Would I get a Cup-winners' medal to go with it?

During the build-up to the Final, nine year-old Andy Kershaw began to collect all manner of pertinent material. It seemed appropriate to announce the coloured section of this book with this splash of colour from that summer when he became a Saints fan.

Final

Wembley   **1 May 1976**

**MANCHESTER
UNITED 0**   **SOUTHAMPTON 1**

Stokes

Att: 100,000   Referee: Clive Thomas

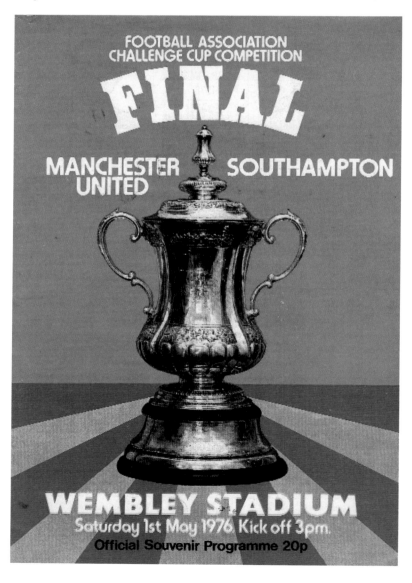

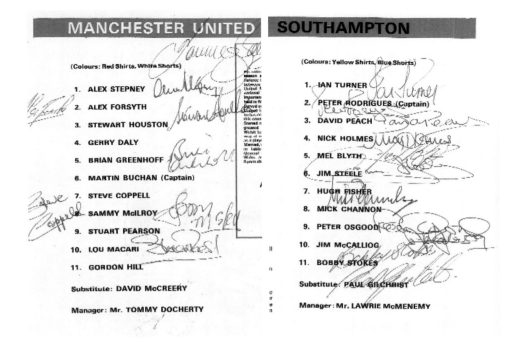

MANCHESTER UNITED

(Colours: Red Shirts, White Shorts)

1. ALEX STEPNEY
2. ALEX FORSYTH
3. STEWART HOUSTON
4. GERRY DALY
5. BRIAN GREENHOFF
6. MARTIN BUCHAN (Captain)
7. STEVE COPPELL
8. SAMMY McILROY
9. STUART PEARSON
10. LOU MACARI
11. GORDON HILL

Substitute: DAVID McCREERY

Manager: Mr. TOMMY DOCHERTY

SOUTHAMPTON

(Colours: Yellow Shirts, Blue Shorts)

1. IAN TURNER
2. PETER RODRIGUES (Captain)
3. DAVID PEACH
4. NICK HOLMES
5. MEL BLYTH
6. JIM STEELE
7. HUGH FISHER
8. MICK CHANNON
9. PETER OSGOOD
10. JIM McCALLIOG
11. BOBBY STOKES

Substitute: PAUL GILCHRIST

Manager: Mr. LAWRIE McMENEMY

Team Changes

UNITED	No changes	
SAINTS	7 Gilchrist	12 Fisher

Highlights

Turner made early saves from Hill, Daly and Pearson.

20-yd shot from Gilchrist forced save from Stepney.

Saints won first corner of game when Forsyth put behind under pressure from Stokes.

Coppell brought down by Holmes. Forsyth drove free-kick into wall.

33 mins: Channon put through by McCalliog but Stepney saved.

HT 0-0

60 mins Rodrigues concussed near half-way line, then McIlroy headed ball from corner against angle of post and bar.

Channon and Osgood worked chance for Rodrigues, but shot well wide.

67 mins: Hill replaced by McCreery.

United won two corners in rapid succession.

83 mins: 1-0 Channon flicked on to McCalliog who put **Stokes** through to score with early shot past Stepney's left hand.

FT 1-0

And so it came to pass that Wembley Stadium experienced its first-ever invasion from Southampton.

The players' wives and girlfriends had a head-start: they had travelled up on the Friday, stayed in the *Royal Garden Hotel* in Kensington and had then gone on to the stadium, knowing that they would not be united with their partners until after the match.

Footballers' Wives ain't what they used to be. The players' wives and girl friends arrive at Wembley in trouser suits presented to them jointly by Bass Charrington and a Portsmouth boutique. Nobody seems able to recall who presented the teddy bear being cared for by Jane Channon, kneeling at the front with Anne McMenemy.

Back in Southampton, meanwhile, they were putting on their colours for the day – and that included plenty who didn't have a ticket but who were just seeing off those who did. For the lucky ones who were Wembley-bound – survivors of overnight ticket-queues, flights from Australia and goodness knows what else – it was a question of choosing between the special train-service or joining the convoy of cars and coaches on the M3.

For a couple of supporters, however, the skies beckoned. Desmond Goodenough, a restaurateur in Ampfield, and his friend Alan Grant paid £150 each for a champagne-and-caviar return flight by helicopter. Lyndhurst-based Grant, founder and captain of Rumbridge Pack Rugby Club, left his team-mates to host 50 French rugby players from Le Havre.

The two of them also managed to provide a ticket to the match for their pilot and Saints fan, Capt Michael Bell.

All aboard the chartered flight from Ampfield to Wembley.

All dressed up but no ticket to go

Opposite: Having failed to get a ticket, Mr H. Verrall – the *Echo* caption-writers were less informal with their use of forenames in 1976 – put on his gear, added his own signs to those at the Chilworth roundabout and waved off those with tickets.

Above: This off-to-Wembley photo shows (*left to right*) Ethel Hedges, niece Christina, daughter Elaine, family friend Sarah and husband Charlie. It probably wouldn't strike you that Sarah wasn't going to Wembley: she was not a fan, but felt obliged to dress up and see off her friends.

Editor's note: *Elaine wonders whether her father, Charlie – now 94, but still a regular at St Mary's – is the oldest surviving fan from Saints' May 1976 visit to Wembley. We are not aware of any claims to the contrary, but I do know that he is not the most senior citizen to have been to the subsequent Charity Shield match: my dad, who is eight months older than Charlie, sat out the Final but joined me, in the August, for the 1-0 defeat by Liverpool. I now await irate letters from insulted centenarians, waving tickets and rosettes.*

On the march: getting there...

The coach left at 8.30 and had various pick up points around the city. Yet it didn't take too long to reach the first pit-stop at Fleet Services on the M3 *(pictured below).*

What struck me was the number of coaches there, with Saints fans in Cup Final regalia and the huge amount of yellow-and-blue, mixed in with red-and-white striped shirts and scarves. The invasion was on. There were huge jams on the North Circular and, with the first sighting of the Twin Towers, a massive chorus went up of

Que sera, sera.
Whatever will be will be.
We're going to Wemberley

... and we really were.
Nigel Hale

I was 10 and went on the coach with my brother Matthew, our next-door neighbour, Ray Garvey, and his son Patrick. My mum packed home-made burgers in baps, which were fantastic. We sat for ages on the steps leading up to the turnstiles before going in to the stadium. I had something bubbly on the return coach. I think I lost my home-made rosette a few seasons ago, but I still use my scarf when we play in yellow-and-blue.
Julian Sutton

I took the SFC-chartered special train. The atmosphere built from the moment we left Southampton to the moment we pulled into Wembley Central. *I'd Rather Be A Devil Than A Saint* (to the tune of *El Condor Pasa*) crowed a cocky young Man Utd fan, pointing his finger in an aggressive manner. He must have been waiting at the station exit just for me to happen along.
Chris Newman

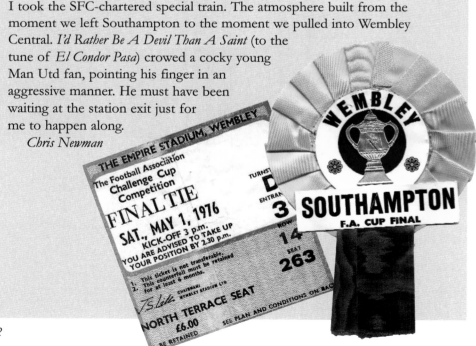

At the team's headquarters, meanwhile, Nick Holmes was trying to keep his feet on the ground. Like thousands of others around the country, he had acquired, young, a Cup Final-day routine. He sat down in front of the TV and watched every minute of the coverage from the build-up, with *It's A Cup Final Knock-Out*, through the interviews with the teams at their hotels and then following the progress of the team-buses up Wembley Way. Apart from toilet-breaks, he wouldn't move until the last post-match interview from the bowels of the stadium was ended.

So, now that the 21 year-old local boy was actually going to *play* in the game, he was in no doubt that he was about to experience "something very special". He was also quite clear about what he wanted to do on that morning.

> The people from *Grandstand* came to do interviews at the hotel and I remember thinking that I really didn't want to do that. Fortunately, Ossie said he would speak for me. All I wanted to do was play football, which was the only thing I thought I had a chance of doing properly. Now it is the kind of thing I would probably flow through and enjoy, just like Ossie and Mick did on the day.

For those Saints fans lucky enough to be going to Wembley in those pre-video recorder days, it would be many years before they got the chance to see the pre-match interviews. But most of those who watched at the time must have been struck by the marked difference in composure between "the underdogs from the South coast" and the "red-hot favourites" as more than one newspaper identified the two sides. Despite the optimism of their former hero Bobby Charlton, who was quoted as saying that his old team would score six, it was fairly obvious that the Reds looked extremely nervous, whereas the Southampton players seemed unperturbed. That point was not missed by Peter Rodrigues, as he prepared for the afternoon ahead: "we were relaxed but not over-confident in the morning. Barry Davies was interviewing us and then they crossed to the United lads who, to us, looked very tense."

Ian Turner confirms the confidence that was running through the side.

> There were things that had happened all the way to Wembley that I took as signs it was to be our year. A rare goal for Hughie in the Third Round, Jim scoring with his head in the replay and a ball coming back off the post and into my arms in the Fifth Round all made us believe we could win it. We were confident and I 'phoned my brother and told him to put some money on us.

The degree of confidence they felt was not just blind optimism. They had prepared well and Lawrie McMenemy had done his homework, aided by those scouting missions by Ted Bates and Bill Ellerington, who recalls that "the only thing we were worried about was if they got a quick goal. We thought if we could hold them for 20 minutes, we could do it." Channon drew a similar message from the reports on United: "they were enthusiastic; they were busy; but you could stop them. If you could stick out the first 20 minutes, you had a chance."

My day started at about 6.00am. We wanted to get to Wembley early, as my friend Andrew's father had a room in the *Wembley Conference Hotel*, after a meeting in London. So we were able to watch the build-up on TV, before making our way to the stadium.

The Cup Final *Grandstand* showed the Southampton Ladies winning their FA Cup. It was the sixth season of the Women's competition and the fifth time they had won it. What we didn't know, of course, was that this would be the first occasion that a city would claim both trophies.

Although massively outnumbered, the Saints fans sported a defiant banner – YELLOW AND BLUE VERSUS MANCHESTER WHO? – a riposte to Gordon Hill's arrogant words after the semi-final [see page 56, if you need reminding of them]. When Hill was replaced by McCreery in the second half, it settled the matter: his post-match interview after United's semi-final win was to be his last significant contribution to the tournament.

After the players' lap of honour, I was disappointed that they disappeared back into the tunnel so quickly and that the adventure was over. When we went back to the hotel to check-out, Andrew and I met Kevin Keegan, who was a member of the BBC panel covering the game. "How do you fancy joining Southampton, then, Kevin?" I asked. Four years later, of course, he did; and when I later met him as a Southampton player, I reminded him of that conversation.

"I knew that someone must have put it in my mind," he said.

Steve Eckersley

And the way to stop United was to stop their wide men. This was the focus, Rodrigues recalls, of the reports: "it was the wingers – how to stop them playing, basically – and they got it right." It all added up, Channon suggested in his autobiography the following year, to "the greatest bit of tactical scouting I have ever known."

While pleased with the "excellent" scouting reports he had received on all six rounds, McMenemy recognised that he had available, for the Final, another source of low-down on the opposition. Having benefited from Mel Blyth's inside-knowledge of Crystal Palace, so he could now turn to Jim McCalliog for an analysis of the club he had played for until just over a year ago.

> We were training for the Final and Lawrie asked me if I had anything to say about United. I told him that we had to watch out for them all coming out fast behind a good clearance. What we would have to do is make sure Ossie came out with them.

The United back-four could also be expected to move up sharply when the Southampton defence fed the ball up to the their midfield, he explained, so as to restrict the opportunity for a through-ball to an on-side runner – advice which, as it turned out, McCalliog himself would crucially have to follow.

All of the planning and psyching-up was momentarily disturbed as the team-bus approached the stadium. A fan stepped off the pavement and into their path. "We all jumped up," Rodrigues recalls, "and the lads were very concerned. When we got to the dressing room, Lawrie said 'settle down lads; I'll go back and make sure everything is OK.' Well, he went back and everything was OK, so then it was a case of let's get on and prepare for the game."

Settling in to the dressing room was an evocative occasion for the 52 year-old Ellerington. The holder of three England caps at schoolboy-level and two as a full international, Bill had never represented his country at Wembley. But his surroundings set him thinking about the history seeping from the old concrete walls and how far he had come.

> I walked around the dressing room, thinking about all the great players who had been in there. It was amazing. I had been at the club since 1940, so it meant so much to me – and Ted, too, of course. I had started at Sholing Boys School, then moved to Sunderland, my father's home-town. My father was an ex-pro [who had guested for Saints during the First World War]. When I got my Schoolboy caps, the scouts were looking at me and I signed amateur for Sunderland. Then, in 1940, we moved back to Southampton.
>
> We had a visit from Tom Parker [the manager], who asked me to play for Saints. All the pros were in the police or working in factories, so I signed amateur. Tom used to collect soldiers on Salisbury Plain, to make up the numbers. I eventually went into the RAF as aircrew and, after demob' in 1945, I rejoined the Saints, but the club were fined 30/- [£1.50], because I was still signed to Sunderland.

On the march… stadium encounters

The coach was waved in among all the Southampton coaches, we were told to remember where it was and then we headed off.

First impressions included the overwhelming smell of the hot dog and burger vendors, with their vastly inflated prices, and the number of MU fans, many of them sitting around, sipping on cans of bitter and lager. Bearing in mind the reputation of United's following in the mid-70s, it felt slightly intimidating. We made our way along Wembley Way up towards the stadium concourse, exchanging pleasantries with the opposition, who made remarks about country yokels (thankyou, Mick) and how many goals they would stuff us by. I remember thinking they were over-confident, but didn't exactly say so. After what seemed like an eternity, we got to the top of the Wembley Way – a mass of United red-and-white (*above*).

Nigel (*left*) and Craig

We turned left towards the Saints end, pausing for a photo in front of the Twin Towers (*left*). It was a lot quieter here, after the bustle of Wembley Way. Once inside the stadium, we were in the huge concourse area and paused for some liquid refreshment. Again, we were surrounded by MU fans, many of whom were the worse for wear and slightly abusive. Given that Craig, the youngest member of our party, was only 10, we didn't hang about but made our way up the stairs to our standing area. The view, the colour and the noise that greeted us as we entered the arena was

brilliant: Saints fans were already singing their hearts out and the yellow-and-blue colours – in balloons, banners, beanies and top hats – I will never forget (*right*). The green pitch seemed miles away and I remember thinking that where it started was further away from us than the Milton Road end, if you were standing at the Archers end.

Nigel Hale

On the march: stadium encounters...

Having made a few financial sacrifices to secure some of the best seats in the stadium – no standing on the terraces for this match; this was to be a family day-out to be remembered – I remain disappointed that my many happy – nay delirious – memories of the day should ever have been tainted by a jobs-worth steward.

As our party of four – my wife, our two children and I – approached the turnstile, this steward stepped in front of us, hands held high. He glared at my young son, bedecked in a yellow-and-blue scarf and rosette and holding a tiny Saints flag, purchased only a few minutes before from one of the myriad of colourful and persuasive vendors around the stadium. "You can't bring that flag in here," he bellowed at seven year-old Ian. "Why on earth not?" I enquired. "It has a stick in it and that is an offensive weapon," our intrepid steward explained. But we were at the game as a family, we were not hooligans and, I further pointed out, we were in a "Saints fans-only" part of the stand. I accepted it might conceivably have been used as an "offensive weapon" outside the ground, where the two sets of supporters were in close proximity; but inside, sitting alongside fellow-Saints fans? No way!

Unmoved by my reasoning and protestations, the steward began to assert his authority by raising his voice: "either you hand over the flag-stick or you will not be allowed in." Reluctantly, I took the flag off of the offending stick, which was all of 18 ins. long, and handed it over. As we went through the turnstile, with Ian forlornly holding a flag he would not be able to wave, the steward called after us to inform us that he would be at the gate at the end of the game and we could retrieve the stick.

Think about it: goodness knows how many of the 100,000 crowd would be exiting – emotions high, win or lose – through his particular gate, this steward assumed we might seek him out to get our 18 ins. stick back. What for? To use as an offensive weapon, as we met up with United fans outside the stadium? The man refused to think or act logically. His was the triumph, my son's the disappointment.

It did not, however, spoil our enjoyment of the game: as a family we did indeed have that day out to remember. And there was time for Dad to install a substitute-stick for the celebrations on the Sunday.
    Herbie Taylor

Herbie's party : Naomi, Nicolette and Ian, the next day,
after the flag had had a quick fix with a new stick.

While Ellerington was reflecting in the dressing room, the players were making the traditional inspection of the pitch, dressed in beige suits supplied by Squires boutique in Above Bar. Holmes retains a particular memory of that moment: "you remember odd things about the day. When we went on the pitch in those rather gay suits, I remember someone spitting at me." A fashion critic, possibly?

The players come out, in their "gay suits", for a pitch-inspection.
Left to right: Peach, Gilchrist, Rodrigues, Turner, Holmes (out of spitting range and waving), Earles, Bennett

If the clothes were a little bit dandy, Channon dispels the myth that Saints approached the game in a cavalier manner and insists they were well prepared.

> We always knew we had enough ability to win it. It all came together in the Cup run and on the day of the Final. People say we didn't do tactics, and there were some players that you wouldn't tell how to play, but we were well set-up for the Final, defensively, and we knew we would have to be patient. We couldn't leave ourselves wide open, which was probably our biggest fault normally – all we wanted to do was score goals – but it was such an important game, that didn't happen. Cup Finals are all about winning – not how you play.

By now 27 and with 31 England caps to his name, Channon was in his prime. But he was conscious that, for some of his older team-mates, this Final "was a last chance. When they talked about Manchester United being a First Division club, we knew we had far more experience than them – and, in the likes of Ossie, better players too."

Before the month was out, Mick would be captaining England against Italy in New York, but Ellerington was able to look back to the time, 12 years earlier, when he was a scrawny teenager playing for Wiltshire schoolboys. Bill has often been credited with discovering Mick, but rejects that simplification.

Nobody finds a player. There are always people watching. Anyone who claims to have discovered a player is lying, because all the scouts talk to each other. So, although I was the first to see Channon, he had been recommended by the school-teacher. Ted Bates sent me to see Wiltshire schoolboys play Hampshire schoolboys at Andover's ground. He wanted me to look at young Channon. It was a drizzly night and he was running all over the place and enjoying himself. I went back and told Ted I liked him because of his enthusiasm and also because he always attacked the defender by running at them with the ball. I knew, as a defender, that they hate that.

As the time came to walk up the tunnel, McMenemy's work was largely done. He and his staff had got the players ready and, once again, he had reminded them of which team had the most experience, listing games played and international caps won by the players on each side. With his words ringing in their ears, Ian Turner believes they went out feeling they had nothing to lose.

All Lawrie drummed into us was not to let ourselves down and that was the attitude. We were prepared to lose if we played well and then we would have held our hands up. What we didn't want was to get beat and then sit in the changing room, regretting what we could or should have done.

So what thoughts were uppermost in captain Rodrigues's mind as he led the team out into the sunlight? Immense pride at skippering a Cup Final team, tempered with a degree of surprise that a free transfer had ended up working out so well.

As the teams follow managers Docherty and McMenemy out of the tunnel, the Saints are led by
the three players with Cup Final experience: "show us your medals!"
The visible players are (*left to right*) Stepney, Houston, Rodrigues, Pearson, McCalliog, Macari and Osgood.

On the march... stadium encounters

When we arrived at around 11 o'clock, there was a line of parked cars in the middle of the Wembley carpark. Across to the stadium, United fans were milling about in large numbers. We heard that some Saints supporters had been attacked and robbed of their tickets, so we stayed put in the line of cars. This early in the day, there were not many police around.

Phil (*left*) is dressed
(boot and ticket out of sight)
and ready to go, with Tony and Paul.

No way I was going to lose my ticket, so I took off my Doc Martens boot and my long, thick red-and-white sock and placed my ticket on my foot, replacing the sock and boot. I figured that if I did get attacked, they wouldn't find my ticket.

Phil Rawlings

Leaving the stadium, we found ourselves in a sea of Manchester United supporters: for as far as you could see, there wasn't a single Saints fan in sight. There was an awful, stony silence as we were carried along with them and I'll never forget the cold stare of their eyes upon us. We wanted to cheer and laugh, but we didn't even dare smile: we just walked along with our heads down. It's the only time I've ever been afraid at a football match.

Then suddenly I tripped, which made them laugh. We laughed nervously with them and that completely relieved the situation. And soon we were making that wonderful journey back – all the people on bridges, as we got nearer home, waving to us as we drove underneath them.

Elaine Bushrod (née Hedges – see her party's photo at page 71 above)

Without a sympathetic orthopaedic consultant, I might have missed it. I'd fractured my fifth metatarsal, three weeks before, playing football at school – yes, metatarsals were being broken long before Beckham, Rooney and Neville thought of it. The initial prognosis for 1 May seemed poor. But, with a week to go, the doc, when asked a straight question, said that, if the ticket were his, he'd be there, fractured foot or not.

So, throwing away the crutches on the morning of the match, I limped along Wembley Way to my place on the terraces. All was well until Stokes scored. As supporters bounced around in delirium, I stood there like a stork – left foot in the air.

When the coach got back to Bedford Place, I was limping spectacularly and the glory was completed by the looks I got – people clearly thought I was a brave survivor of one of those coach-park battles that had followed the game, as some of United's fans demonstrated their inability to lose with grace.

Mike Sadler

On the march… a halo for Bobby
I wanted to look like "The Saint", with a halo.

My wife said a sheet would be a good idea and she put all the players' names on, with "St" in front.

And she fastened the halo with a coat-hanger and red-and-white tape. Bobby Stokes took my hat with the halo – you can see it in the photographs [as at page 105 below]

I've never seen it since.

George Tomkins

Home thoughts from abroad…
I was managing Ethnikos Pireaus [between spells as Saints' Assistant Manager]. The practice in Greece was, home or away, to go to a hotel, the night before a game, with the squad. We would normally train, Saturday afternoon, and then go on to the hotel to prepare for the match on Sunday.

But I insisted that we went to the hotel, Saturday lunch-time, so that I could watch the Cup Final and then do our preparation for the next day, afterwards. I'd known a few of the Saints side, as youngsters coming through, in Ted's days; and I'd been at Chelsea, as a player, with Jim McCalliog and Peter Osgood.

John Mortimore, President, Southampton FC

I was in Sydney in 1976, in the days before the ethnic station (SBS) provided a live, football feed on TV, for the many migrants from Europe. So I had to listen – at 3.00 am – to the BBC on my short-wave radio, while recording the commentary on my reel-to-reel tape recorder. As always happens with short-wave, the signal used to fade and surge constantly, so listening was a real trial. The goal is – I cannot forget – at the 913ft mark on the tape, which is now in storage in Manchester, condition unknown.

Sean O'Sullivan

But Peter was also thinking slightly more earthy thoughts. In a few weeks' time, he was booked to go to St Tropez with his wife and another couple, with whom they regularly holidayed. In the preceding months, Peter had teased the lady in question – who will not be identified here, for reasons that will become obvious – that she would have to go topless, because "all the women do."

In the week before the Final, Rodrigues had spoken to these friends and a deal was struck. If he did something that demonstrated he was thinking of them, she would go topless that summer. Therefore, he would scratch his nose as they walked onto the pitch. Fortunately, the TV cameras closed in on him just as he kept his side of the bargain, so there could be no doubt. Next time you watch the video or DVD, check it and you will see.

So, was the bet honoured? Pedro just grins and nods.

Once that piece of fun was over, things got serious and Rodrigues's suspicions as to the mental state of the opposition were confirmed when he shook hands with United captain, Martin Buchan.

> When we tossed up, I saw his legs were shaking – and that was a Scottish international! I couldn't believe it. I told one of our lads he was shaking like a leaf. I then thought, "if we can overcome the first 20 minutes, we are in with a shout." They did hammer us for the first 20, but we expected that; but then, after half-an-hour, I thought we wouldn't lose. I knew actually winning would take some crafting, but at least we could hold them out.

Holding them out took some doing at the beginning and Ian Turner looked more than a little nervous.

> In the first 10 minutes, they were bouncing off my head and everything but, as Pat Jennings used to say, "use any part of your body as long as you keep them out." I don't think I ever felt I was having a bad time; I just got on with it.
>
> We thought more about what we were going to do than what they might do. I think we were right not to worry about them. We concentrated on doing our jobs right. I remember we thought that if we all battled, then, if one of us didn't win the ball, somebody else would. That was the way we were. We were so close-knit as a team: we battled for each other and I think that's what won us the Cup.

In front of Turner, Mel Blyth was shouting himself hoarse, as he marshalled the defence.

> Nobody gave us a chance but we had such a lot of experience compared to them. I couldn't see their forwards doing anything because I had played against Pearson and McIlroy a few times and never had too much trouble with either of them.
>
> Bulldog [Turner] took 10 to 15 minutes to settle down – I kept telling him to calm down – but after that I couldn't see them scoring. Mind you, I couldn't see us scoring either.

Alongside Blyth, Steele played the game of his life and he would be named *Man of the Match*.

Mel and I had a good relationship, whereby he attacked the ball and I stood off. I stepped up for offside so many times in the Final, I couldn't believe that Stuart Pearson didn't cotton on. It was so easy. Pedro and Peachie pushed up and frightened their wingers, who had to drop back and mark them. They didn't have a big target man, so Mel won everything in the air. We did have a good understanding and we only let in four goals in the whole Cup run.

Completing the back-four was David Peach, who reckons he had the easier job of the two full-backs: "I marked Steve Coppell and he was pretty direct. So I could rely on my speed. I thought Pedro had a harder job with Hill, who was trickier. I think we both played our part."

As someone who had spent his career cracking open defences, Peter Osgood was probably better qualified to sum up the contribution of the Saints defence.

> They were awesome and the best thing that happened in the build-up was an article in the *Evening Standard* that said our central defenders were the weak link. That wound Steelie up and he could *play*. He was a good player with a great left foot. And Mel was an intelligent player, who was passionate about the game. I think the back-five won it for us.

Once the initial pressure had been dealt with, it became a question of where a goal might come from. Osgood, one of that rare breed to have scored in every round of an FA Cup run (Chelsea in 1970, in his case) had been playing deeper since the autumn – a change of formation explained at page 136 below – and had not scored in Saints' run.

Although without a Cup goal since the Fifth Round replay, Channon was still Saints' top-scorer (with five) in this run and fancied by the fans – with their JESUS SAVES – CHANNON NETS THE REBOUND banners – to make it six

Despite his deeper role, Osgood was still expected to compete in the air – as in this duel with United's Greenhoff.

or more. But when he found himself through on goal, with only Alex Stepney to beat, his attempt to "shove it by him" was foiled by the 'keeper's toe.

A disappointed Mick defended himself in his autobiography.

> A lot of people say I should have lobbed him but I don't think so. I thought I had done the right thing at the time, because Alex hadn't spread himself and, the way the ball was bouncing, I couldn't have flicked it over him with any confidence.

Channon has only Stepney to beat, but he will have to settle for the five goals he had by then scored in the run.

And so half-time arrived with no goals. Back in the dressing room, McMenemy was his usual calming influence. The skipper recalls that the half-time instructions "were to carry on as we were: continue to keep Coppell and Hill quiet – which we did – and the chances will come." Peter Osgood likewise applauded the way the manager handled it all.

> Lawrie told us to keep playing the same way and chances would come. The pitch was superb and we were a good footballing side. Lawrie was really accurate in telling us how it would go and instilled confidence in us. He was superb.

As the hour-mark approached, it was still goalless, but that was within the first-hold-them-then-hit-them basis of the side's planning. Bill Ellerington can "remember looking at George Horsfall a few times during the game, because we both knew that, as time went on, if we didn't do anything stupid, we could win it." But then there was a scare. Rodrigues took a blow to the head and was concussed for the next few minutes. While he was still recovering, United won a corner, from which Sammy McIlroy headed against the woodwork.

Before the corner was taken, the sponge was squeezed on the back of my neck. I found out later that my mum, watching at home, thought the water was blood coming from my ear and went loopy. When the corner came in, I was struggling to jump and ended up wrapped around the post. It was a turning point but, at the time, that doesn't occur to you: you just carry on playing.

Turner was largely unfazed by the whole incident. He had "gone near post" as the ball came over from the corner and across to the far post: "by the time I turned round, it had hit the bar and was coming back."

Soon after this, Tommy Docherty withdrew Hill and sent on David McCreery. The psychological importance of the Doc's decision shouldn't be underestimated, particularly as far as Rodrigues was concerned: "when Gordon Hill went off, my chest puffed out because I knew it was a case of job done. I thank Paul Gilchrist for that, because he protected me that day. I did my job, but Gillie helped."

Turner, having "gone near-post," turns to see an unmarked McIlroy heading against the woodwork, as Rodrigues, recovering from his knock on the head, "struggles to jump".
Left to right: Peach, Turner, Holmes, Macari, Rodrigues, Gilchrist, Blyth, McIlroy, Coppell.

It seemed, with just seven minutes to go, that extra-time was going to be needed to separate the teams. Paul Bennett, along with Bill Ellerington, was "just going to see where we could get some tea," when they were halted by the moment all Southampton fans had waited a lifetime for. Just as McCalliog had predicted, the United defence had held their line.

When the ball came to me from Mick, they were coming out and, as it was coming to me, I could see Bobby on the left, calling for the ball. I just lifted it into the area where he was. I knew they would come out and they did. Bobby had timed his run and it worked nicely. It was never offside, because Bobby was going forward as I played the ball.

The Saints bench was directly behind Stokes as he took his shot early and the ball bounced past Stepney. Ellerington, his quest for a cuppa put on hold, recalls that, "when Bobby's shot was half-way there, we knew they would be picking it out of the net." It was a "tremendously proud" moment for the old-stager who had played with Stokes, 27 years his junior, in the "A"-team.

Holmes still had enough energy to reach his team-mate: "I'm pretty sure I was first to Bobby when he scored and the feeling of joy stays with me. Then I think we all felt this was our destiny and we never felt threatened in the last seven minutes." The pictorial evidence confirms that Holmes was, indeed, the first on the scene. Rodrigues was almost certainly last, but he was determined to get there.

Above: Bobby Stokes completes the Channon-McCalliog move as those two team-mates stand and hope. *(Left to right.)* Channon, Daly, Greenhoff, Blyth, McCalliog, Stokes.

Below: As Stokes (mostly hidden by Greenhoff) wheels away, you can see, through the netting, that the linesman's flag is down.

I ran 40 yards to get to Stokesie. As a schoolboy, I loved Brazil and, whenever they scored, the full-back always seemed to appear in shot about five seconds later. We were playing in Brazil's colours and this was my chance to act out the schoolboy dream, so I ran to him and jumped. Then I had to get back and, when I did, I thought about how long there was to go. People expect me to say it was the longest seven minutes of my life but it wasn't, because we were completely in control. We carried on and played the same way and I knew we would be safe.

Holmes has recalled correctly. He was indeed the first to grab Stokes, with Peach (No 3) in second place. Steele (No. 6) and Channon (No.8) compete for third, but McCalliog opts to race after Coppell (*left*) to seek his reaction: "Stevie, Stevie, what's the score?"

He was clearly more confident than his goalkeeper who reckons that "when the goal went in, that was the moment when I knew we would have to really battle and then came the longest seven minutes of my life." When those seven minutes had almost ticked by, David Peach found himself near the referee.

> The ball went out of play and Clive Thomas said, "How do you feel, Dave?" I told him I was done for: "how much longer to go?" He said "you've just won the Cup Final" and blew his whistle. I just fell down on the floor and then Ian came over. Then I was fine and the celebrations started.

As goalkeepers tend to do, Turner and Stepney had a moment together: "Alex Stepney congratulated me and we put our arms round each other. And Tommy Docherty was tremendous in congratulating us." You can evaluate how magnanimous that was of Docherty if you read his foreword to this book – with the accompanying photo – and appreciate how deflated he was. Blyth can likewise "remember Tommy Doc being terrific, telling me I had stopped them all day. It still makes me emotional." Mel had almost lost his voice from constantly shouting to Steele to "keep it tight" but claims he "knew" they wouldn't score – and "at the final whistle, the adrenalin meant I felt I could fly."

With the game won, Peach had time to reflect.

> We weren't lucky. We had some really good players: McCalliog was a Scotland international; Osgood, who had been the best centre-forward in Europe; Channon, who was the best centre-forward in Europe, at the time; and Rodrigues, with loads of Welsh caps.
> We knew we could play anyone on our day. After Ian's rocky first 10 minutes, we always fancied ourselves to win it.

And was the goal offside? Not according to the skipper: "if anyone says 'offside' to me, I always tell them I had the medal to prove it wasn't." Picking up that medal, along with the Cup, was the next order of business.

> Of course, the real dream-come-true was picking up the Cup from the Queen. Because I was that much older, I took it all in and I do remember everything,

On Her Majesty's Service

I was working at Buckingham Palace as Press Secretary to Her Majesty The Queen. One of my routine responsibilities was to inform The Queen of the expected media coverage when she was carrying out official engagements.

I sent a note about the Cup Final, mentioning that there would be close-up shots on television as the Cup itself was handed over. In fact, having been a Saints fan since 1945, I wrote "when you present the Cup to the Southampton captain."

Back came the note approving the arrangements, but with the comment that "Edward tells me it will be Manchester United, not Southampton." I was pretty certain that the Prince would be proved right but I was, of course, delighted when that Bobby Stokes goal settled it.

Ron Allison

Prince Edward was wrong: his mother was obliged to hand the Cup to the Southampton captain. A memorable moment to which Her Majesty has not risked an anti-climax: she has never been to an FA Cup Final since.

including being grabbed by the Saints fans on the way up the steps. I always chew gum and I had to get rid of that. Then Her Majesty congratulated me and asked if I enjoyed the match. People ask me if collecting the Cup from the Queen was the greatest moment of my life and I say "no": it was turning left and lifting it to the Saints fans, a few seconds later. That was the greatest moment.

"The greatest moment of my life": Rodrigues "turns left" to display the Cup to the Saints fans.
He is followed (*left to right*) by Turner, Osgood, Gilchrist, Blyth and Fisher.

The wives respond by tossing the teddy bear into the air.
1 Janet Williams (Stokes's girlfriend), 2 Jane Channon, 3 Corinne Gilchrist.

Jim Steele has always seemed a tough, no-nonsense sort of man but, in the moments after the final whistle, he reflected on the personal road that had led him to this point in his life. His description betrays a far more sentimental character than many would expect.

> In my time at the club I had played with so many great players – Terry Paine, Ron Davies, Jimmy Gabriel, Dave Walker, Dennis Hollywood, Eric Martin (who was my running mate) – so it meant a lot to me to win the Cup.
>
> I remembered coming here, because I was supposed to be going to Leeds. I knew nothing about Southampton. Don Revie had watched me in the UEFA Cup for Dundee. He decided I was too skilful for a centre-half and then, all of a sudden, Ted Bates was there [to pay a club-record fee] and I was playing against Nottingham Forest on the Saturday.
>
> I remember my first day and Ron Davies walked into the dressing room and looked at me. He said "are you the new signing from Scotland?" I said I was and he said "that's a lot of money for a freckle." The guys were great in those days. There was a booze-culture, though, and, believe it or not, I never drank until I came here.
>
> You don't really remember the day when you win the Cup. I remember going out on the pitch, jumping up on Stokesie when he scored and going up to meet the Queen – it was drummed into us that you go up the 39 steps, turn left and say "thank you, Ma'am" – but I have to watch the tape to remember much else.

After the game, one of the wives asked what the Queen had on and all I could remember was her gloves. We were filthy and I was frightened to even look at her. The nicest thing was seeing the faces of George Reader and Ted Bates, because it meant so much to them. Their faces were shining.

Hugh Fisher could be forgiven if he had felt sorry for himself, having missed out on the action, but he remains philosophical and sums up the spirit of the team.

The single most important factor in us winning the Cup was togetherness. We went forward as a team and there was no animosity between anyone at any stage. No little cliques. Everyone was mates which stood us in good stead and was our great strength.

And what of Paul Gilchrist who, but for Fisher's lack of full fitness – and utter honesty about it – might have been on the bench?

I remember the day like yesterday, the game and the celebrations afterwards. Pedro told us to take it all in because it would go by quickly. Of course, today the Cup Final doesn't seem so important, but then it was the highlight of anyone's career. I soaked it in and loved it.

The size and passion of the crowd was fantastic. The players love the atmosphere and the noise and if you can get the result for the fans then it is like handing it back to them. I had about 15 family members in the crowd. I did look but I couldn't see them. I saw them afterwards and they seemed more drained than anything.

The lap of honour was different than in previous years, as Don Taylor explains.

The FA allowed the staff to go round the pitch with the players. It was the first time they made the photographers stay in one of six locations round the pitch, rather than following the players on their lap of honour. That is why there were so many pictures with us all in.

Most of the pictures with "all" of them in have one notable absentee in Holmes.

When you see the pictures of the team going round Wembley with the Cup, I am never in them. I was just dead and I was about 50 yards behind everyone. The nervous energy meant I was shattered but I was walking around thinking "this is wonderful".

So, in the end, the side's belief in themselves had been justified. Turner's brother had done well, by the way, to follow Ian's self-assured advice: he had placed a £10 bet and won £55.

It is fitting to leave it to Channon, who had been so confident for so long, to sum up the longer-term significance to the club to which, his restlessness and transfer request earlier in the season notwithstanding, he had remained so steadfastly loyal.

This photo gets near to Don Taylor's recall of "pictures with us all in," in that it includes the two non-playing squad members, sub Fisher, the three coaches, physio and chief scout – everybody except Nick Holmes.

Back row *(left to right):* Earles, John McGrath, George Horsfall, McCalliog, Gilchrist, Bennett (peeping under the Cup), Blyth, Don Taylor, Rodrigues (aloft), Bill Ellerington, Jim Clunie, Fisher. Crouching: Stokes, Turner, Osgood, Steele. Seated: Peach, Channon.

Despite his protestations, Nick Holmes did occasionally sneak into shot, as in this photo of the lap-of-honour. *(Left to right):* McCalliog, Gilchrist, Rodrigues, Channon, Steele, Jim Clunie, Holmes, Osgood.

The great thing is that the people who support Southampton now are the generation who were kids then. And now they are taking kids of their own and that's how it goes on.

Southampton FC will always survive. The ups and downs of football are like life: you have highs and low, but, as long as you keep the young support, you have the continuity for the future.

You support a club from your heart. Anyone can say they support Manchester United or Chelsea, but the people who saw us win that day remember Stokesie, Turner, McCalliog and Channon and pass that on to their kids.

The club will survive because it has a heart. It might take many years but, if they can have another great day like when we all went to Cardiff in 2003, well the kids who were there will remember that and it carries the spirit which is Southampton FC.

It is all opinions as to whether the club is about this person or that person. It really doesn't matter: the heart will carry on.

We were just a part of it.

The man in the middle...

It was a special day because I was only the third Welshman to referee the FA Cup Final. I was called on a Sunday morning by Reg Paine, the Referees' Secretary, to notify me and congratulate me.

I was more than pleased because it was Southampton and Lawrie McMenemy, with whom I had become reasonably friendly, because we respected each other. So that made that Sunday a very important day, but things changed on the Monday morning, when I received a telegram which said "CONGRATULATIONS! YOU'LL DO FOR US. LAWRIE McMENEMY." Some might say that was unprofessional but, to me, it was typical of him, conveying his thoughts of me as a referee and pleased that I was appointed.

Some weeks later, I received the itinerary from the FA. I was surprised to see that, after the match, I was due to be a guest of Manchester United at their banquet. I rang the FA Secretary, Ted Croker, to ask what it was all about. He said this was normal, so I told him we had two guests on the day and I would like them with us in the evening. He referred me to United's secretary, Les Olive, who said it was out of the question: they had no spare tickets. I said to forget it and we wouldn't go. So back to Ted, who said the arrangements couldn't be changed. I asked if we could go with Southampton and he said "No". I said I might just go to the *Talk of the Town* instead, not realising Saints were going there.

He said it was fully booked, but I rang my personal friend, Frankie Vaughan, and he soon had the manager of the *Talk of the Town* on the 'phone, promising a table.

Before every match, I would suggest to my linesmen what I thought particular players might be likely to do: in this game, they would need to look out for possible offsides, because of the pace of the United forwards. I half-expected their pace to overrun the Southampton defence. Players I briefed them on were Macari, who did a lot of yapping, and also Mick Channon. We knew how good he was and how he liked to hold on to the ball; and we liked to look after footballers and ball-players. Peter Osgood had a lot to say, but he was a 100 per-center. The FA tried to stop me doing this, because they thought I was prejudging teams and players, which I disagreed with.

At the start of the Final, I was presented to the Prime Minister, Jim Callaghan, who was from a Welsh constituency in Cardiff; the Saints captain, Peter Rodrigues was Welsh; and, of course, there was a Welsh referee. Never in Cup Final history had such a thing happened.

United didn't play well, but I don't think it would have made a difference if they had because, on the day, Southampton played the best I'd ever seen them play. Channon was outstanding. Peach and Rodrigues were outstanding in defence, where you also had Jim Steele, whose name was entirely appropriate: it was the way he played. What I liked about him was that, if he was going to hit the player, he just hit him. As a referee, if you could stop him prior to the act, you were OK but, if you couldn't, you had to deal with him. But I had enormous respect for him. He was outstanding in the Final. He wasn't that fast. Pearson was fast. Macari was difficult to get off the ball and Hill and Coppell were all fast. Jim could have had a difficult afternoon, but he was outstanding.

When Bobby Stokes scored, I wasn't in the best place to judge, but he looked offside. I looked over to my linesman, who had no doubt about it. I told him afterwards that it looked tough to give. He said "No, it wasn't tough: he was onside." In fairness, there was no appeal from the defence. Years later, though, and after seeing it many times on TV, Tommy Docherty said to me that it was possibly offside, but it didn't worry me. The game itself was easy to referee and I had no problem with any of the players. After the match, when I watched them being presented, I took a moment to reflect on the Welsh issue and to feel very proud.

I spotted, in the crowd, the elderly gentleman who used to look after the visiting officials at The Dell. These are the things that mustn't be forgotten in football. There was a family atmosphere at Southampton - always a cup of tea and a sandwich, as soon as I arrived. I always found it to be an extremely friendly club. Not all clubs are like that: some are too large to be that friendly.

When we got to the *Talk of the Town*, there were police on horseback outside. My wife thought it might be because of my performance, but I assured her I had had an OK match. We went in and, to my amazement, Lawrie came up and put his arm round me. *Match of the Day* were there and I received more money from the BBC for appearing than for refereeing the Cup Final.

Clive Thomas

We didn't feel pressure, because we were a young side at the time, so it wasn't really a pressure-situation. Although there was an expectation, it wasn't really pressure.

Looking back, I'd have to say we were nervous. My lasting memory of the Final is being so dry all the time in my mouth, which was obviously a nervous reaction. We didn't have enough knowledge, back then, about the importance of drinking water regularly and, all game, I was as dry as a bone in my mouth.

I have the video of the game at home but I've never ever watched it. But, in my mind's eye, I didn't think I played very well – so that must mean David Peach had a good game.

Watched by referee Thomas, who was surprised by the dominant Saints defence, Coppell again finds Peach having "a good game".

The next day, we went back on the train and had a civic reception at the Town Hall in Manchester, where Tommy Docherty promised the crowd that we would go back the next year and win the Cup. At the time, all the players were thinking "why don't you shut up, Doc?" But in some bizarre way, it became the focus of our season, the following year.

Steve Coppell

We froze. If you were to speak to any player who played in that Final, they'd tell you the same thing. The game was just a non-event: we never performed. I suppose experience told at the end of the day. We were a very young side. We were probably a bit too cocky as well. They had a lot of experience in the side – Peter Osgood, Peter Rodrigues, Jim McCalliog, Micky Channon – and, on the day, they did the business.

It was a terrible thing at the time, but I suppose the better side won on the day. We couldn't believe it. We were young and we thought all we had to do, really, was to go out there and we'd win. But it wasn't the case. They did the business – and we lost.

Gerry Daly

On the march: home triumphant

Dad and I were completely euphoric as we left the ground and made our way across the coach-park, but were brought abruptly back down to earth by the marauding Mancs, who were stoning any opposing fan they could get close to.

But we sang our coach back to Wickham Square, where sandwiches had been laid on in the *White Lion*. We didn't have replica shirts in the 1970s, but you can see, from the photo, that my dad wore a home-made yellow-and-blue one.

Glen Williams

Glen (*right*), with his dad, Stan (in D-I-Y shirt) and cousin Mark (a Chelsea supporter) celebrating in the *White Lion*.

Just to prove he still has it, Chris Newman obliges, 30 years on, with a photo

The Cup Final "Special" rattled back into Southampton Central around 7.30 pm. The streets outside were complete bedlam. I've not seen anything like it before or since. Car horns blared in a constant, rhythmic cacophony and people danced in the middle of the road. Some of the stationary vehicles ended up with Saints fans, bedecked in club favours, clambering up on to their roofs.

I bought a red-and-white flag – complete with Saints' crest – from a street vendor outside the station. That may seem like an odd thing to do on the way back from a game, but then the driver of the bus I travelled home on wanted to keep it in his bus window for the rest of his duty. No chance! In fact, I still have it.

Chris Newman

Walking home to Chiswick, West London, at about 7 o'clock, I passed a couple of kids playing in the street. As one of them kicked the ball, he added his commentary: "…**and it's Stokes!**"

Andrew Wrigley

More from the other side...

You might wonder what excuses I'm going to put forward ... I'm not – I'm just going to admit that, ... on the day, we didn't do ourselves justice ... For the first ten minutes or so, ... there seemed to be more than a touch of desperation about Southampton's play.

There was, perhaps, also a hint of fear. But as the game wore on ... experienced men like Peter Osgood, Mike Channon and Jim McCalliog finally started to make things tick for the Saints, and I have to admit that, right through the game, Southampton had big men at the back in every way, in Peter Rodrigues, David Peach, Jim Steele amd Mel Blyth. ...and when Southampton began visibly to muster increasing confidence, the signs were there they could snatch victory.

If a goal is awarded by a referee, it stands, whether you think it's offside or not. And I'm not going to start any arguments now about the one which Bobby Stokes tucked away for Saints ...

I would not want anyone to think that I am giving Southampton little credit for their performance. They did the job in the best way they possibly could, and they did it effectively.

Lou Macari

In other news...

An earthquake struck the northern Friuli region of Italy. Eleven villages near the Austrian and Yugoslav borders were affected in what was Italy's worst-ever earthquake. At 6.5 on the Richter scale, the quake left 550 people dead and 80,000 homeless.

In the following 12 months, hundreds more quakes occurred and damage was estimated to reach £3,000m. Tent cities were eventually replaced with 20,000 pre-fabricated houses, but the Italian government was severely criticised for the time it took to carry out the reconstruction.

Prime Minister Giulio Andreotti would visit the region in the autumn to be greeted by angry protests. By the end of the year £250m of European Community donations had been spent in rebuilding the region's infrastructure and rehousing its inhabitants.

James Hunt won the first of his six Grand Prix victories in the Formula 1 season in Spain. He would go on to be crowned World Champion driving a *McLaren-Ford.*

While the players and officials of Southampton FC were celebrating in the Guildhall, and many thousands of Southampton's residents were gathered outside, ITV was screening *From Russia With Love*, starring Sean Connery as James Bond.

Cup-Run Appearances

	Aston Villa	Aston Villa replay	Black -pool	West Brom	West Brom replay	Bradford City	Crystal Palace	Man Utd	Games Played
Turner	1	1	1	1	1	1	1	1	8
Rodrigues	2	2	2	2	2	2	2	2	8
Peach	3	3	3	3	3	3	3	3	8
Holmes	4	4	4	4	4		4	4	7
Blyth	5	5	5	5	5	5	5	5	8
Steele	6	6	6	6	6		6	6	7
Fisher	7	7	7	7	7	7	12	12	6
Channon	8	8	8	8	8	8	8	8	8
Stokes	9	11	11	11	11*	11	11	11	8
McCalliog	10	10	10*	10	10	10	10	10	8
Gilchrist	11*	12		9	9	4	7	7	6(1)
Earles	12			12					0(1)
Osgood		9*	9			9	9	9	5
O'Brien			12		12	12			0(2)
Bennett						6			1

* indicates player substituted
12 (bold) came on as sub
12 sub did not come on

Goals: Channon 5, McCalliog 3, Stokes 3, Gilchrist 2, Fisher 1, Peach 1.

Let's Party!

After the match, there was a reception in the Wembley hospitality lounge. It was an opportunity for Chairman George Reader to say a few kind words to Paul Bennett.

> He was brilliant. He said he was sorry I hadn't played because he knew it would have meant so much to me as a local lad. It was very thoughtful and I appreciated that.

It gave some of the players their first chance, post-match, to meet up with their families, although some of the wives and girl friends headed straight back to their hotel. Sandra Earles recalls that Bobby Stokes's girl friend, Janet Williams, was singing the 1962 hit, *I Want to be Bobby's Girl*. And why shouldn't she?

Mel Blyth and his wife skipped these preliminaries, as they had more pressing matters to attend to: 17 days-old Kelly needed feeding, so they rushed home, en route to the evening's festivities at the *Talk of the Town*, where the entire party, backroom-players and all, assembled for the official, post-match celebrations.

Keith Honey feels that the club looked after his back-room staff "well", but a few of the players found the choice of venue strange. Nick Holmes thought it "a bit of a disappointment": as a Southampton lad, he "would have rather been back

Left: *Bobby's Girl*, Janet Williams, gets to hug the Cup, while the 83rd-minute hero gets to wear the lid.

Right: Keith Honey, happy that this his back-room staff have been well-rewarded by the club for their efforts, takes his turn, at the evening's celebrations, to grasp what it was all about: Southampton's FA Cup.
He is joined by Mick and Jane Channon and by Tony Sealy, a 16 year-old Reserve
who would come on as a sub in the Saints' next Wembley Final in 1979.

in the city," although he is quick to point out that "the next day made up for that." Paul Bennett, another local, felt the same: it was as if the venue been booked as a London night-out for the losers.

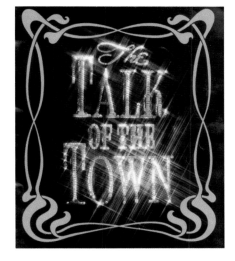

Indeed. But Jimmy Hill and the BBC *Match of the Day* crew could hardly have been expected to follow this team of upstarts all the way to Southampton for two or three interviews: it made their life so much easier to waylay them at the *Talk of the Town*. The goal-scorer and the manager took centre-stage. Hill pointed out to Stokes that he had put four shots in during the match. Looking rather sheepish, Bobby quizzically repeated the number: "Four? In a Cup Final – that's great. No, I'm pleased for the boys, really." Surrounded by "the boys", he predictably suffered hoots of good-natured derision.

Hill then turned to the manager's wife: had Anne McMenemy ever "felt the big man sinking a little bit," earlier in the season, when he had been under pressure? It could have been no surprise to anyone that she "always believed he had what it takes."

McMenemy himself talked about what a "smashing day" it had been, but made two interesting comments on his team's Cup run. Firstly, as already noted (page 57), some of his players may have been "less than choirboys at times," but he'd really had "very little trouble with them." Secondly, he criticised the national "writers and the pundits… they don't see us enough. They watch the First Division and I think we surprised them, but I was very surprised that some of them didn't even ring me this week."

Surely not expecting such an attack, Jimmy Hill laughed. But Lawrie wasn't letting go.

> I'm serious, Jim. They didn't even come to see me and I couldn't accept this at all. I only hope they don't explain it away by saying Manchester United didn't play well.

But, then, we have already seen that Tommy Docherty was making no such excuses and McMenemy confirmed what the Doc has reminded us of in his foreword to this book: that he had 'phoned to offer his congratulations. Lawrie told Hill that Docherty and United had been "tremendous".

And so the news, from the *Talk of the Town*, was official: Southampton was the talk of the country – and deservedly so. The players had had, Peach reckons, "a smashing night, but it wasn't what you'd imagine it to be. We were relieved and knackered and had a quiet evening with our families at the *Talk of the Town*. And then I slept with the medal under my pillow."

It is hard fully to describe in words what happened in Southampton the next day but, for the benefit of those too young or too far away to have witnessed it, we hope that the pictures on this and the next few pages – some of them professional but several of them contributed by fans who were there – will help them to appreciate the nature of the revelries that some described, Dave Juson reminds us in *Match of the Millennium*, as "wilder than VE Day."

Scenes from the bus tour

(anti-clockwise from the top)

Thornhill: Dave Webster photographed the delayed bus "speeding up" along Hinkler Road, where he lived: "not only had we won the FA Cup, but it went past my front door."

His father, Ken, had made his own "replica" for a group-photo in the garden.

Back row (*left to right*): Ann Hillier (auntie), Malc Hillier (uncle), Chris Webster (Mum), Mark Webster (brother, in Saints shirt), Dave, John Webster (uncle), Julie Webster (cousin), Doreen Webster (auntie), Brenda Cull (cousin). Front: Ken Webster (Dad, with Cup), Matt Webster (second cousin, on bike).

Shirley: The bus reaches the junction of Burgess Road and Hill Lane.

Waiting for them there were the Warren children, Peter (*left*), his sister Judith and cousin Keith. The family group to the right of them provides another example of the improvised placards that marked the occasion.

Having picked up the Sunday 'papers before going to bed on Saturday, Peter Rodrigues had begun to "realise that we had done something very special." On Sunday morning, Peggy Worlock and others from the party "took a walk around Kensington Palace," before boarding their designated coach – the players were still travelling separately from their ladies – for the drive back to the South coast.

It was an "incredible" journey, Paul Bennett recalls: "it really started to build up at Basingstoke and the crowds on the bridges told us we could expect something a bit special when we got back." Rodrigues was almost mesmerised by the trophy.

> I sat with the Cup on the bus and couldn't take my eyes off it. By the time we got to Eastleigh, the crowds were gathering beside the road and then we got to the *Ford* factory and there were thousands of people there. Bobby's medal went missing for about 20 minutes, but there was no panic: it was just being passed round by all the people who wanted to see it.

The diversion via Fords had not been planned, but the message reached Lawrie McMenemy that, if they didn't swing by, then mass-absenteeism was likely to close the factory for the day. The reception they received there gave some idea of what was to follow. After stopping at The Dell, they switched to an open-topped bus, for their unforgettable tour of the city. Some of them have recalled what it looked like from the top of the bus:

Peter Rodrigues – When I lost in the Final with Leicester in 1969, there were about 7,000 people there when we got back. I thought that was quite good, but this was something else. The trip around the city was fantastic and, although everyone wanted to hold the Cup, I didn't want to let it go.

I remember asking Steelie where we were and he said "Shirley". I didn't recognise it for all the people and the thing that struck me was how many were shedding a tear when I held the Cup down for them to touch.

Gilchrist is behind a row of Steele (*left*), Rodrigues (not letting go of the Cup) and Peach. In front are Stokes and McCalliog.

Ian Turner – It was funny because, as we went round the town, we did see people we knew in different areas. My digs were in Bitterne Triangle and I saw people there – it was a strange feeling.

David Peach – I will never ever forget it. I don't believe any Cup-winning team ever had a homecoming like it.

Nick Holmes – I think we were all shocked by the reception we got. The trip around town was expected to take half-an-hour, but it lasted half the day. At one point, in West End, they were trying to speed us along and one of those wires across the road nearly took Jim Clunie's head off.

Mel Blyth – I drove to Southampton on the Sunday and joined the bus at The Dell. I have never seen so many people or so many tough, 6ft-men, kneeling and weeping in the street.

On the way down, I got to the Hill Lane round-about and I got stuck in traffic. I was hooting the horn and one chap got out of his car to give me a mouthful. When he realised who it was, he started getting the cars out of the way, so I could get through and I ended up with a police escort.

These are the things you never forget.

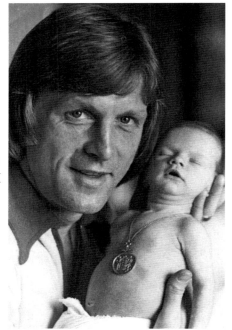

Before rejoining his team-mates, Blyth had a Sunday morning photo-call – Kelly was modelling his medal.

Mick Channon – Winning was great, but the best fun was the day afterwards, back in Southampton. We'd had a great night but we were drained after a long build-up. The atmosphere with the tour round the city was something that you'll have for the rest of your life.

Paul Bennett – The route that the bus took through Millbrook, where I had lived, and past *The Saints* pub, was incredible. Guildhall Square was a memory that will stay with me forever. When we turned left off New Road and then right by the cinemas, the numbers of people were just astonishing.

Pat Earles – It seemed all my old school-friends [from St Mary's] were out there. It did make it very special for me.

Peter Osgood – I've never seen scenes like it. It was brilliant after we won it with Chelsea, but somehow we were expected to win things, whereas Southampton had no expectation. I believe everyone wanted to be a part of it because they knew it might never happen again.

Osgood and his kiss-blowing manager as the bus passes through Shirley.

"The numbers of people were just astonishing."

There were various estimates of the crowd in front of the Guildhall but it seems likely that more than 200,000 people gathered, some of them with precarious viewing points. Rodrigues witnessed one moment of near-tragedy.

> When we got to the Guildhall, the crowd was incredible and I saw a guy fall from a balcony. He was lucky as he landed on a shop awning and was unharmed, but the memory stays with me. Then I heard a noise: it was the boats in the port tooting.

Another reception followed in the Guildhall and it was time to take off all the scarves and hats that had been thrown to the players. Rodrigues was told to take off his red-and-white hat by one of the Directors: "quite correctly, he pointed out that was no way to meet the Lady Mayor."

Once inside the Civic Centre, Chairman George Reader had a quiet word with Jim McCalliog. On the previous Saturday he had featured in a newspaper article, headlined *Jimmy Mac gunning for the Doc.*

> He told me he was really pleased with me because, after the article, he thought I might stick two fingers up at Tommy Docherty in front of the Royal Box. I told him winning the match had been enough for me and that said more than anything in reply.

The balcony at the Guildhall is certainly not big enough for a whole football team to make an appearance together, so they went out in twos and threes.

There was a special cheer for the trio who had been dropped for over-celebrating after the semi-final and particularly when Peter Osgood suggested they were all drinking milk that evening. Next it was the turn of the Saints captain.

Going out on the balcony made me realise what it was all about. Two months later, as a PR gesture, we went back and replanted all the roses that had been trampled by the crowds.

The City of Southampton honours the achievements of a fine team.

SOUTHAMPTON 1976 F.A. CUP

Guildhall, Southampton
Sunday, May 2nd 1976

Menu

The Hayling Island Three *(left to right,* Steele, Osgood and McCalliog) play from the gallery, with a sip of what Ossie assured them was milk.

Bobby Stokes, sporting the halo bestowed upon him by George Tomkins, whose wife had made it for him to wear to Wembley (as seen at page 81 above), acknowledges the crowd.

After Rodrigues had embraced the mayor, Mrs Elinor Pugh, she began her speech to the crowd. A somewhat boisterous response was quickly subdued by McMenemy – if he had told them to jump, the only question would have been "how high?" – and she then proceeded to bestow the Freedom of the City on Southampton Football Club. It was a grand gesture and one that suited the occasion perfectly: the award ceremony could wait until November.

The crowd then slowly dispersed and the players, directors and staff enjoyed the reception. Not that it was the day's final celebration for David Peach.

I lived at Lordswood and, after the Guildhall, I wanted to have a quiet drink with my wife. So we got a taxi home, intending to pick up our car and go out to the New Forest. When we came round the corner, the whole street was out waiting for us. They had decorated our house and we had a big party.

The prime instigator of this event was neighbour, Jim Dolbear, but his efforts to decorate the front of the Peaches' house had expanded as others arrived with bunting, flags and other bits and pieces. MAGIC DAVE said one banner – it was Peach's "favourite word at the time," Jim explains. He recalls greeting his surprised neighbours: "When I got to Dave, we hugged each other and he said 'it hasn't affected me until now, but now I'm crying.' We all had a really good night. It was a lovely ending to a weekend that will stay in the memory forever."

Except that the "weekend" would be extending into Monday, thanks to Mick Channon. He had arranged his testimonial – Saints v QPR – for that evening: "I was very lucky with my timing," he says of another remarkable evening of celebration and emotion. All the normal rules of stewarding and safety went out of the window: 15 minutes after the kick-off, fans were being ushered around the pitch to sit in front of the walls and Dave Juson has described, in his vivid account of the evening, how, in the second half, this supplementary crowd had spread into the netting, behind Phil Parkes, the visitors' 'keeper .

Officially, the crowd was 29,528, short of the 31,000 capacity, but those who were there formed the opinion that the gate must have been much bigger. In any case, it meant net proceeds to Channon of £15,000. A piffling amount in today's monetary values, to say nothing of football's own bizarre values. But it would have bought Mick *three* cars of the kind that Ford presented to Bobby Stokes for scoring the winning goal.

The motor company had offered the car to any Southampton player scoring a Final hat-trick, but had quickly decided to change those terms. Bobby was the only member of the team who couldn't drive, but the *Bitterne Park Academy of Driving* stepped in with an offer of free tuition.

It was appropriate, on this evening of carnival, that Bobby's £4,500-worth of silver grey saloon car should be parked on the pitch, before the kick-off, with a big "L" on the roof. And the *Daily Express* joined in the fun by presenting Channon with their *Footballer of the Year* award, for which their readers had voted.

Channon also resumed, for the evening, the captaincy that he had voluntarily ceded to Rodrigues six months before when, having asked for a transfer, he "didn't think it was right, wanting to move and being captain." Having thus had the honour, by default, of receiving the Cup from the Queen, Rodrigues was only too pleased to hand back to Mick for the evening:

Above:
The prize-winner and his car: Stokes shows he is ready to learn.

Channon's testimonial was, of course, perfect timing. You couldn't wish for a better guy to have that stroke of luck. He was my room-mate throughout my time there and gave monumental service to the club. He thoroughly deserved it.

The quality, let alone the result, of the football match was almost

Mick Channon last night... showing off the Cup and the Express trophy to the fans.

Your Footballer of the Year gets 30,000 cheers

Left:
The *Daily Express* photo and headline announce the man with two trophies to show off.

incidental, though it should be recorded that QPR were top of the League but waiting for Liverpool to play their final match to see who would be Champions. Liverpool would beat Wolves, the following evening, and take the title.

Bobby Stokes, having got into the habit, scored both Saints' goals, with Frank McLintock and Peter Eastoe netting for Rangers. Peter Osgood always believed he scored the winning goal but the referee, Alan Robinson, disallowed his shot. The ref seems to have offered two reasons for this: that he had already blown for full-time; and/or that the shot had hit a spectator on its way past Phil Parkes. If that seems pathetically lacking in clarity and conviction for a referee of repute, it should perhaps be borne in mind that Mr Robinson was from Waterlooville, where the locals followed a team who had not won the Cup since 1939.

As the visiting defenders prepare to walk off, leaving the six-yard box to goalkeeper Parkes, Stokes (No. 11) and invading spectators, referee Robinson blows his whistle before any of those invaders can come between Osgood's shot and the goal.

Having invaded the pitch as Osgood's shot was goal-bound, the crowd then refused to leave until the players had made an appearance in the Directors' Box. Afterwards, there was yet another reception to attend, this time at the *Royal Hotel*.

That was not the end of the partying as, pending their celebratory holiday in Barbados, the players were being asked to attend other functions – from a meet-the-public gathering in *Debenhams* to visiting a neighbourhood where they had baked a cake. The *Echo* declared Southampton THE CUP CITY and printed car-stickers to that effect, while cars sporting yellow-and-blue ribbons remained a common sight – for at least two years, it seems.

Above: When they held a celebratory tea-party for 126 children in Magnolia Road, Merry Oak, there was a 22 ins. cake with four miniature footballers on it. So four live ones came along to cut it.
Left to right: Gilchrist, Turner, Fisher, Bennett.

Below: If you've not seen this 1976 sticker in any cars or bedroom windows for a while, we recommend you look out for it next time you're in Oslo. When Saints fan, Brian Smith, had visitors from Norway – brother-in-law Len and nephew Andrew – the week after the Final, they took this souvenir home with them. It has remained, ever since, in Andrew's bedroom window, even though he has long been a professor in Trondheim.

We come from ~
SOUTHAMPTON
THE CUP CITY!
Home of THE SOUTHERN EVENING ECHO

Mike O'Brien of *Hammond's* Jewellers in Shirley was summoned to The Dell to collect the plinth of the FA Cup.

> I went into the board-room to find Billy Dainty, Bernard Breslaw and Leslie Phillips, who were all appearing in Bournemouth and who had been invited to view the Cup. I noticed there was no lid on the trophy. We eventually found it in the boot of one of the players' cars.

If nine year-old Andy Kershaw appears
transfixed as he gazes at the FA Cup,
on display at the Art Gallery,
that's because of the impact that
the summer of celebrations
was having in defining him as a Saints fan.

Hundreds of fans went to The Dell
to be photographed with the Cup
and Lawrie McMenemy.

Below: It looks as though this was
the 274th photo-opportunity.
Ian Gordon, a third-generation Saints fan
(and nowadays a director), with his
wife Carole and fourth-generation Robert.

Bottom left: Ted Bates gets himself
a private session on the pitch.

Left: Peggy and Monty Worlock have their
private photo-call in the boardroom.

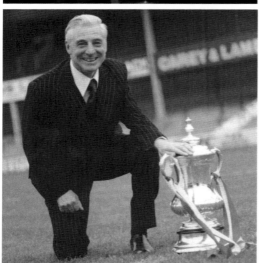

The engraving was carried out by Mr Bastin and there was also a small dent to be removed. Nobody ever admitted to damaging the Cup, but Peter Osgood happily admitted to taking it out one evening to the *Tiberius* casino and later drinking tea from it at a burger van on Commercial Road. That story has been much-repeated but it omits to mention that a radiologist, who was in the casino, borrowed the Cup for half-an-hour and took it to the Southampton General Hospital, where he X-rayed it. Although it is among the mass of memorabilia we have to hand, we regret that this X-ray seems incapable of reproduction here – to say nothing of what terms the FA might impose on our exhibiting an X-ray of its trophy.

O'Brien declined McMenemy's offer to put the Cup on display for fear of any harm coming to it, but he did ask and obtain George Reader's permission to cast silver and gold miniatures as charms which retailed at £10 and £75. And the Cup did go on display in the Art Gallery for a while and fans could have their photo taken with it at The Dell.

Then the players had their Barbados holiday. They didn't all go, though. Mel Blyth stayed behind, not just to watch baby Kelly grow into his medal but "because I was getting my nose fixed." Paul Bennett did go and played in both of the exhibition matches.

> One game was on the Barbados Bridgetown Test-cricket ground. The square was so hard nobody worried about what it might do to the pitch. I was kicked by one of their forwards and Steelie, who was playing slightly the worse for wear, went after him.

Pat Earles also travelled and played on this "wonderful" tour: "a number of fringe players got to play, Malcolm Waldron and Manny Andruszewski included. Playing on the cricket ground was quite unusual."

Still living in South London, Blyth was, and is, regularly reminded of what had been achieved.

> I had Saints supporters who lived there pinning cards on my front door. I had a telegram from a chap on the *Queen Elizabeth* congratulating us. I still get people bringing me programmes to sign. I have met people in *Tesco* at Purley to sign a programme – and it goes on.

It does indeed go on, as the researching and writing of this commemorative book has demonstrated. Those "Boys of '76" who participated in the Cup run, including the bit-players who were – and still are – made to feel part of it; those working behind-the-scenes, some of whom made it onto the "bench" at Wembley; and "Lawrie's Army" of fans, some of whom have contributed their memories and memorabilia to this 30th anniversary tribute, have all reminded us – and you, too, we hope – how and why 1 May 1976 was the single most important day in the history of Southampton FC.

Paul Bennett had left by the time the rest of the Cup Final squad came to be photographed with the Cup and three Reserves, each of whom would soon get a start in 1976-77, with varying degrees of success.

Back row (*left to right*): Don Taylor, Steele, Blyth, Osgood, Andruszewski, Jim Clunie.
Middle row: Williams, Gilchrist, Middleton, Turner, Channon, Holmes.
Front: Fisher, McCalliog, Rodrigues, Lawrie McMenemy, Stokes, Peach, Earles.

Only the late Bobby Stokes was missing – and missed – when the other 13 members of the Final squad were joined by manager McMenemy and trainer Clunie for a 25th anniversary dinner on 28 April 2001.

Back row (*left to right*): Lawrie McMenemy, Jim Clunie, Bennett, Gilchrist,
Blyth, Osgood, Holmes, Fisher, Channon, Steele.
Front: Turner, Earles, McCalliog, Peach, Rodrigues.

The Boys of '76

This section focuses on what happened next to "The Boys of '76."

We have defined those "boys" as the 15 players who took any part in the Cup run. That includes Gerry O'Brien who, having been transferred to Swindon in the week after the Sixth Round, was not part of the 14-man squad for the Final (pictured *opposite* at their 2001 reunion dinner) and who might reasonably be described as "The Forgotten Man" of the run to Wembley.

That said, the section is effectively in two parts:

- ◆ The 12 players who received medals: the 11 who played at Wembley, plus Fisher, the non-playing substitute.

  Their stories are arranged in shirt-number order, save that the captain comes first. Each tale is headed by a signed, coloured picture from the 1975-76 season or the following one.

- ◆ The other three players: Bennett, who played one whole game; and the two who came on as subs – Earles (once) and O'Brien (twice).

  Each of their stories is headed by a black-and-white photo.

Bobby Stokes's story is derived from four interviews: one that he gave to the *Topical Times Yearbook* early in the 1976-77 season; and three with his team-mates, conducted by Tim Manns in 2005-06.

The remaining accounts are all based on interviews conducted exclusively for this book – often supplemented, in respect of careers elsewhere, by information from club historians listed in the "Acknowledgements" and, in a few cases, by histories cited in the "Sources": Hereford (Gilchrist); South Africa (Blyth); and Southport (Fisher).

Peter Rodrigues

As club captain, Peter started the next season, as expected, in the first team. While some of his Cup Final team-mates were struggling to keep their places, he was ever-present – along with Channon and McCalliog – until the end of October, when his run was halted by an injury in training.

> I twisted my ankle in a tackle with Mel Blyth but then, in frustration, I kicked the ball and made the damage much worse. Basically, I knackered the ligaments in my right knee and, from that point on, I struggled to keep my place.

Although he would be 33 come January, Peter knew that he could, if fully fit, command a place in the team on merit. With a knee that wasn't working properly, it was a different story. He managed just six more games, in three spells, the final flurry of which began with a 2-1 defeat at Nottingham Forest, in which he scored the last of his three goals for the club, and climaxed in a Good Friday farewell against Plymouth Argyle at The Dell, when he was substituted during a 4-1 win.

He admits that, as a player, "you always want one more season and it takes someone else to tell you when it is time to stop. In the summer of 1977, Lawrie offered me a free transfer but I decided to quit playing completely." The great irony was that, after a three-week break, he found his knee had recovered. But the decision was made. A few weeks at Romsey Town was followed by two years in California, firstly coaching and then spending a year out of the game.

> I came back and didn't want to be one of those ex-players who hung around their old club but Nick Holmes asked me to come to a match against Liverpool. I went into the players' lounge with the likes of Ian Rush and Kenny Dalglish and felt comfortable knowing that I had made the break and wouldn't be thought of as a hanger-on. At that point, I knew it would be all right to come back and start watching the game.

As so many players did, Peter was looking at the licence trade. He had already considered this in Sheffield before joining the Saints, so it was the obvious thing to do when he finally retired from the game. He bought the *King Rufus* in Eling, with some helpful advice from director Basil Bowyer, and spent six months doing the place up. The opening in December 1977 was a great success with plenty of fans queuing up to see the Cup-winning skipper, but he knew it would need good beer to keep them coming back. For good measure, he also provided a friendly atmosphere – with the added bonus of his football memorabilia on display.

In 1987, he decided it was time for a change, sold the pub and spent ten months painting and decorating for a friend. He and his wife, Lin, soon found that they missed the licence trade so started looking for another pub.

The *Whitemill Inn* at Whitemill, near Caernarfon, was exactly what they wanted. Yet, even after two years there, Peter felt that he was still viewed by some as an outsider, mainly, he believes, because he doesn't speak Welsh.

So he demanded silence across the bar, one evening, and pointed out that he had sung the Welsh national anthem 40 times, when being capped by Wales, despite not speaking the language. He was, and is, proud of his Welsh heritage and was quietly amused to find that two of the locals who had led the whispering campaign actually couldn't sing the anthem themselves.

Ever "proud of his Welsh heritage", Rodrigues joins fellow-Welsh internationals (and fellow-Saints), Ron Davies (*right*) and Ernie Jones at the *Dell Diamond* launch in 1998.

He had made his point – and he knew that some of the locals respected him the more for doing so – but the die (or Dai) was cast and it was time to move on. Returning to Southampton, they started a venture each: Peter ran a café, while Lin had a shop selling wedding dresses in Hythe.

These enterprises were less successful and Peter was soon managing the Shirley Conservative Club. He stayed for eight years – until Lin died in 1998: "it was obviously a very difficult time and I found I couldn't stay in that job. I needed a complete change. Spain seemed to offer me the break I was looking for, but I missed Southampton and life in this country."

Doing up the *King Rufus* – with a little help from his friends.

After spending the early part of the new decade in Sax, north of Alicante, he came back to Southampton and is now happily settled in Regent's Park with Kate, who had arranged the flowers at his wedding to Lin. He has a driving job, which he really enjoys, and he finds he is often asked to reminisce about winning the Cup.

I could probably do my job in half the time if it wasn't for regular requests for the stories about those great days playing for Southampton. I find the fact that people still want to hear about it, 30 years on, simply amazing. One of my customers caused considerable consternation by complaining about me, but it turned out to be a big joke as his complaint was that he was a Manchester United supporter and he didn't appreciate regular visits from the captain of the Saints.

In 2004, his daughter Amanda decided to sell his Cup Final medal at auction. This caused a rift with Peter that he doesn't believe will be healed. He is very happy that Southampton FC bought the medal (*above*) and that it is on display in Reception at St Mary's.

The two programmes, below, illustrate Ian Turner's considerable tour of local non-league clubs (itinerary *opposite*). Thus he played fairly regularly for Salisbury in 1984-85 and began the 1987-88 season as manager of Brockenhurst, for whom he made a change-of-programme appearance in a pre-season friendly.

His next tour was of hard-hat locations, latterly with UK Construction, as seen here in 2004.

Ian Turner

Although he would be at the club for another two years after winning the Cup, the turning point for Ian was the first match of the new season. He injured his left knee and needed an operation to remove both cartilages.

For the next three months of League games, McMenemy turned to Steve Middleton, his young Reserve 'keeper, and two short-term loans, Colin Boulton and Jim Montgomery, with Turner making three convalescent appearances in Europe – both First Round legs of the Cup-Winners' Cup against Olympique Marseille, in September; and the away leg, in November, of the Anglo-Italian Cup in Napoli. The loan spells over, Ian managed three League games before McMenemy made a permanent signing, Peter Wells from Nottingham Forest. Wells played every match from then to the end of the season.

Ian started the next season, 1977-78, in the first team and kept his place for eight League matches before Wells took over. Another four-game spell ended with a 2-3 home defeat to Millwall. It was February and third-placed Saints were heading for promotion. But Wells now became first-choice keeper and that was that for Turner.

After half-a-dozen games on loan at Newport County, he was transferred to Fort Lauderdale. Having enjoyed summer football – "I had a good time out there and felt fit" – he came home in October 1978. Initially loaned to Lincoln City, he joined Walsall in January 1979. After further loan spells with Luton Town (for whom he never started) and Halifax Town, he left the professional game in February 1981 and cut practically all his ties: "to watch never interested me."

At the incredibly young age, particularly for a goalkeeper, of just 28, Saints' Cup-winning No.1 found himself playing non-league football and needing to make a living outside the game. This he did by working as a plumber and pipe fitter for BP, while engaged in some permutation of playing, coaching and managing at Witney Town, Salisbury City, AFC Totton, Waterlooville, Romsey Town, Brockenhurst and Newport (IoW).

Subsequently, his work in the oil industry has taken him to Pakistan, Oman and Libya but he has now settled in his native Yorkshire. His home is near Stamford, although his current job with UK Construction has meant working in the Home Counties, latterly Kent.

His two sons, Liam and Mark, don't play football and when they first saw the Cup Final video couldn't quite believe their dad's hairstyle. These days, Ian shaves his head – "for my work" – so they were delighted to discover that he was once a fashion victim.

The proud owner of a twice-broken nose, Ian has never considered an operation to have it fixed: "That costs money. I'm from Yorkshire."

David Peach

David has never had any difficulty remembering the details of his career, thanks to the kindness of Saints fan, Jim Dolbear, whom he met soon after arriving at The Dell. They became the best of friends but David was astonished, the Christmas after his retirement, to receive a remarkable gift from his friend.

> He gave me five scrapbooks, one of which had the cuttings from the complete 1976 FA Cup run. He had even written to the newspapers in Gillingham and also Bedford, where I played boys' football, to collect cuttings going back to when I was 15. He must have spent fortunes buying all the papers. It was unbelievable.

The scrapbook of the Cup run was started after the replay at Villa Park because, according to Peach, Jim had a vision that the Saints would get to the Final.

There were more highlights to come in David's career with the Saints. He won England U-21 caps and a call-up to the full England squad when they toured South America in 1977. He can count himself unlucky not to get a game.

He and Nick Holmes would return to Wembley as the only survivors of the Cup Final team to play in the League Cup Final in 1979. That was to be his last big occasion with the Saints, although there was one more milestone to achieve. The following August, at the start of his final season with the Saints, he scored a penalty against Manchester United, which earned him the title of highest scoring full-back in Football League history.

Eight months later, his time at The Dell was at an end. David signed for Third Division Swindon Town for £150,000. It wasn't a good move and a free transfer, in March 1982, took him to Second Division Orient.

This meant that he had left a side on its way down to the Fourth Division for one that was dropping down to the Third. He remained at Brisbane Road for the following season, during which his left-flank partners included 1976 semi-final adversary, Peter Taylor, and he became the only player in the Football League, at that time, to have played on every one of its grounds.

At the end of that 1982-83 season, he decided he "had had enough of the full-time, professional game. I was 33 and I wasn't getting any better as a player. It was becoming a bit of a drag." Assistant manager, Frank Clark, who was taking over as manager, offered Peach a coaching job but he "wanted to stop, so they agreed to cancel the last year of my contract."

Over the next eight years, he held a range of playing, coaching and managing roles at Andover, Wellworthy Athletic, Christchurch, AFC Lymington, Dorchester Town, Bashley, Poole Town and Lymington Town, as well as being the technical director with the Bournemouth FA.

But David knew it was time to get, as he describes it, "a real job". An interest in a fish business in Lymington didn't work out so, with the help of Jim Dolbear, he began a new career in the building industry. Initially, he worked as a labourer but, after shadowing two friends who were tradesmen, he started to acquire the necessary skills to move into site management, working his way "through the trades, picking people's brains as I went, until Jim helped me get a job as an assistant site manager on a project in Southampton, working for *A&B Homes*."

Eventually, he became a site manager and is now with *Miller Homes*. He enjoys the work and sees many similarities with football.

> Managing a building site is like managing a football team. You are all lads trying to do a job and working together. You have a bit of the craic, although that is much less evident than it used to be. The main thing is the team-spirit, which all footballers miss when they leave the game.

He also believes that building companies, much like football clubs, tend to offer a pay rise only when the employee threatens to leave for another job.

David lives in Milford-on-Sea with his wife, Joyce. Their son Daniel is an electrician and their daughter Laura works for the St John's Ambulance service.

During David Peach's spell as manager of Christchurch FC, Chris Nicholl – whose Southampton career was just about to end – took a strong side there for a friendly. Nicholl's exciting front three of Le Tissier, Rod Wallace and Shearer (3) got the goals in a 5-0 win.

Although no longer selling fish, Peach still likes to catch them, with a consortium of lake-fishing friends.

Nick Holmes

Nick was the player who lasted longest at The Dell after winning the Cup; indeed, he is third behind Terry Paine and Mick Channon in Saints' all-time appearances list. He was to play in the 1979 League Cup Final and the losing FA Cup semi-finals of 1984 and 1986. And his last-ever start would be the first leg of the 1987 League Cup semi-final.

The defeat by Everton at Highbury in 1984 was the most devastating of his career: "It was such an unjust result but it was Everton's year, just like 1976 was our year. It was terrible. I don't think I ever felt so bad on a Sunday after a game. I remember going to Mudeford and walking and feeling totally empty."

After that game, the team went on a run of six wins and three draws to finish second in the First Division. It was the club's highest-ever finish and Nick deems it the greatest achievement in his career. When he looks back he is also convinced that his arrival in the first team, which coincided with a golden period in the club's history, led by Lawrie McMenemy, could not have been better timed: "I was just lucky. Lucky as hell. I was just born in the right place at the right time with the right people around me. It was wonderful and I loved every minute of it."

When a pelvic injury forced him to retire in 1987, his friend Graham Daish, who was running East Cowes Vics, asked him to turn out for them. He obliged but only briefly: "I did enjoy it and I scored a few goals for them, which for me was unusual, but I had other things to get on with in my life."

Holmes left the Saints with a promise from then manager, Chris Nicholl, that there would soon be a job for him. So he took a year off and then, true to his word, Nicholl invited him back in a coaching role. The job consisted of looking after the Reserves, with George Horsfall, and overseeing the scouting complex.

It was quite a task really, which I did for a year. I am not mercenary but I told Chris that I wouldn't be able to survive on the money they were paying, so eventually I had to go off and work on my own commercial venture.

With the benefit of hindsight, he recognises that, within a couple of years, Sky was putting so much money into the game that his circumstances would probably have been entirely different. He believes he would still have been in the first-class game, but is entirely happy with the way his life has panned out.

He took over the village store in Middle Winterslow, near Salisbury. It proved busy and profitable. Nick had no problem with the long hours: having been brought up with his parents in a newsagents business, he knew what it meant to get up at 4 a.m. to help them do papers. "It didn't worry me to put in long days. It made us a good living and enabled me to provide for the family."

Yet, having settled into what would be the family business for the next 10 years, Nick realised how much he was missing the day-to-day life of a footballer.

It was dreadful. I hated not going into the dressing room in the morning. I missed having the lads around me. That was the hardest thing. It wasn't so much the games I missed as the morning routine with the banter.

A holiday in Florida in the early 1990s led to buying a holiday home. Then, in 1996, the family went to Atlanta for the Olympic Games. While they were there, Nick's wife, Carolyn, became ill with what was eventually diagnosed as Lupus. As the symptoms of this arthritic complaint can be relieved by living in a warm climate, it became obvious that a permanent move to Florida would help her condition: "we set ourselves the task of finding a way to do this, which we did in 1999," in the form of a property management business.

This continued until a friend, visiting from the Salisbury area, lamented Salisbury City's problems. Nick said, almost light-heartedly, that it might be the ideal job for him. Soon after that, Nev Beale, who eventually became City's chairman, rang to see if he was serious. Carolyn knew Nick was unhappy in property management – it "just isn't me" – so they decided he should "come back and see what it was all about."

Nick quickly saw the potential of the club, so decided to try and run his property concerns from England, while getting back into football. It took a couple of years before it became obvious that he needed to be in both places simultaneously. Recognising that he had to resolve the property business, he offered to resign from Salisbury City. But the club opted to keep the job open while he went back to Florida and sold his company. That left the way clear to take up the reins again in Salisbury in early 2005 and Nick believes he is now applying much of the knowledge – and the principles – that he acquired in his years at The Dell.

Even when times were bad, we still had a family atmosphere and nothing went outside the club. That is how it is at Salisbury City. I love it here. I'm not manager of a glamorous football club but I am happy here – just as I was at the Saints, which meant so much to me. My life really has been Southampton and Salisbury, with Florida thrown in the middle.

Nick and Carolyn live in the village of Palestine, near Andover. Their eldest son Matthew plays for Salisbury, their daughter Kimberley is studying Maritime Law at Southampton University and their youngest son Nicholas is at college in Nebraska.

Manager Holmes (*left*) with his jubilant Salisbury players in February 2006, after their 1-0 win at Stalybridge Celtic in the Third Round of the FA Trophy

Mel Blyth

By the end of the 1976-77 season, seven of the 12 players from Saints' Cup-winning side had played their last game for the club. Blyth was the seventh and, in his case, it happened after "a few words" with the manager about breaking up the Cup-winning team too quickly.

> We're mates now, me and Lawrie. At the time, I thought he'd done it too quickly. I think in retrospect he'd agree with me now.

Terry Venables took Mel back to Crystal Palace on loan in November 1977, when Ian Evans suffered a broken leg. A transfer to Margate during the summer of 1978 was soon followed by a call from former Palace coach George Petchey who was, by then, manager of Millwall. A move followed and Mel finished his League career at The Den.

As so many footballers did, he then travelled. He had had a taster, in the 1978 close season, with Cape Town City, then being managed by his sometime Crystal Palace coach, Frank Lord. The club had imported several other ex-Football League players, including Mel's former Palace team-mate, Mick Hill. Lord now brought in four guests, Blyth being joined by Mick Channon (then at Manchester City), Kevin Keegan (Hamburg) and the Ireland striker, Mickey Walsh, a member of the Blackpool side Saints had beaten in their Cup run. Those three were each committed to a month's stay, but Mel had a three-month contract in Cape Town, on a football scholarship sponsored by *Mobil Oil* (see the photo at page 18 above).

His next overseas jaunt was to the USA with the Houston Hurricanes, followed by a year in the Far East. He signed for Bulova Hong Kong in September 1981, along with Charlie George – who had been released by Southampton – and Barry Daines from Spurs. In Mel's case he was on a two-year contract but, halfway through, he came home for the birth of his second child Michael and decided not to go back.

His manager Ron Wylie was desperate for Mel to return but he'd had enough. His refusal brought his playing days to an end in a quite dramatic fashion: "They cancelled my registration so I couldn't play over here. Charlie, who had taken me to the airport, was 'phoning me every day, saying they were calling me 'the ghost'."

For that year when his playing registration was cancelled, the pro game was not an option but, in truth, that didn't really matter.

> I never wanted to go back into the game professionally. I know what most players are like and I knew I'd be thinking what they were going to do before they did. I had a young family and wanted to spend more time with them. My first club,

Scunthorpe, offered me a management role but I'd had enough, although I was flattered that they thought enough of me to make the offer. After all, I had only been with them for a year, way back in 1968.

Mel's career outside football has included a building firm and a driving school, but he takes the most pleasure from coaching in schools three days a week: "I absolutely love doing the coaching with kids."

The pro game did eventually draw him back when he accepted a match-day role with the Press Association, through the PFA, 'phoning in match statistics. Throughout his time at The Dell, and when playing overseas, Mel's home was always in Sanderstead, near Croydon and he hasn't strayed far since those days. He now lives in Wallington, Surrey.

He is an honorary member at Selsdon Park Golf Club, in the grounds of the hotel where the Saints had prepared for the Cup Final. Mel still enjoys the occasional round, if not at the standard he played in his Palace days. When the Scottish full-back, Davie Provan, moved from Ibrox to Selhurst Park in 1970, with his family still in Glasgow, he had Blyth playing four or five times a week: "I actually managed to get down to scratch for a while," Mel recalls.

Much of his spare time nowadays, though, is devoted to his grand-daughter, Danielle, "who I adore." Danielle is the daughter of Kelly (who can herself be seen – aged 18 days and wearing Daddy's medal – at page 102 above).

Mel Blyth returns

Above: His second coming at Crystal Palace, 1977

Left: He occasionally revisits Selsdon Park – where Saints prepared for the Final in 1976 - for a game of golf.

Jim Steele

Of all the players in the team, Jim is arguably the one with the most reason to look back with at least some measure of regret for the lack of further success and achievement in the game.

Blessed with an abundance of ability and yet teak hard – when compared to more recent players, Roy Keane springs to mind – he would be finished with the game in England just a few days after his 27th birthday. Not that Steele admits to any regrets. He has always been far too busy enjoying life and the company of friends to reflect for too long.

Less than six months after winning the Cup, McMenemy loaned him out to Glasgow Rangers. Jim hadn't wanted to go but believes that Lawrie was trying to change things and that he had no choice but to go to Ibrox. The manager there was Jock Wallace, who did not appreciate the clever flourishes that Steele's admirers associate with his play.

"It was an absolute nightmare," says Jim, recalling the game in which he signalled to a "horrified" goalkeeper to "roll the ball to me". Whereupon he "jinked past" the opposing centre-forward and started the move that led to Rangers' opening goal. Yet, "at half-time, Jock told me not to take the ball from defence but to leave it for the 'keeper to kick it out because he could clear it 80 yards forward."

Things didn't improve and, when it came to the Old Firm derby, he was astonished that the team talk consisted of the chairman, Willie Waddell, reminding the players who the opposition were and then saying "No Surrender".

We got beat 1-0… and surrendered!

After five games, of which the Celtic match was the only defeat, Jim couldn't wait to get back to Southampton. He would regain his place back in the side for a run that included five games in the FA Cup – as Saints contrived to replay each of the three rounds they survived for – and the Quarter-Final of the Cup-Winners' Cup

But March 1977 was to be a watershed. Having missed the Fifth Round home draw with Manchester United, through suspension, he returned for the replay at Old Trafford, only to be sent off by Clive Thomas for "persistent infringements", after a series of bad-tempered exchanges with Jimmy Greenhoff. In between scoring both of United's goals in their 2-1 win, Greenhoff had ripped Jim's shirt. That was no excuse, though, for McMenemy, who made no secret of his annoyance with the errant Steele.

Even so, Jim retained his place for the visit, a week later, of Anderlecht, when the Saints needed to recover from a 0-2 first leg defeat. On one of those special, atmospheric Cup nights at The Dell, the match looked to be going into extra-time when Ted MacDougall added to David Peach's first-half penalty with only 11 minutes to go. But then came the moment that has stayed with Jim ever since.

> Van Der Elst came towards me. I went to trap it and it went under my foot. He ran through and scored and, even now, if I'm in Southampton, people ask me if I remember Anderlecht. How could I forget?

Jim admits that, after the game, he and Lawrie fell out. He played one more game, a home League defeat to Nottingham Forest a week later, and then his career with the Saints was over.

In May 1977, he went to America to play for Dennis Viollet at Washington Diplomats, with the intention of spending three months and keeping his fitness up, before returning and continuing his playing career in England. Somehow, three months turned into 18 years, as he continued playing in Memphis, Chicago and Pittsburg – until a knee injury caused him to quit.

> I had the ligaments removed from my left knee and I was told I wouldn't be able to play again, but I found that my thigh muscles were so strong I could get by for a while. I played indoor soccer for about a year but I am paying for it now, though.

Having at first gone back to his original trade as an electrician, he then opened a bar in Washington DC. It was reasonably successful and he gained valuable experience, which he would put to good use on his return to Britain. He left America in 1995 because he wanted to be nearer to his parents in Edinburgh, but he didn't really settle back in Scotland.

So he returned to Southampton, where he started in the licensing trade, initially at the *King George* in Shirley. Then he moved to Woolston, before taking a management position running various pubs. In 2001, he moved to the Cotswolds and, after running a golf club for a year, is now landlord – with his 'other half', Gill – of the *Black Bear* at Moreton-in-Marsh.

The *Black Bear* has become an ideal pit-stop for Saints fans returning from northern venues, like this party homeward-bound from an away win at Manchester City in April 2004. Finding another hero of 1976 there, after a day's golf with the landlord, they then lined up for a photo, against a backdrop of a famous yellow shirt.
Back row (*left to right*): Rob Bryan, Becky Bennett, Jim Steele, Hugh Fisher, Malcolm Ross, Jamie Ross.
Front: David Ember, Richard Ember.

In July 2005, when the Saints were scheduled to play Anderlecht in a pre-season friendly at St Mary's, one of Jim's regular golfing partners, Jimmy Case, rang him to ask whether he was going to watch his 'other' favourite team.

He still hasn't forgotten Anderlecht.

Paul Gilchrist

Lawrie McMenemy laid down a challenge to the players after winning the Cup. There was now promotion to be won and he was giving them the first six games of the new season to prove their commitment to remaining part of his plans.

Paul believes he never had the opportunity to meet that challenge head-on. He played in the Charity Shield, a match which passed him by.

> I cannot remember a thing about it. I never saw anything on TV afterwards and, at the time, after winning the FA Cup, I thought "Great, we are going to go back and do all that again," and it was nothing like it, a real anti-climax. Probably having no memory of it is the best thing.

Then came the first match of the 1976-77 season, a dismal 2-1 defeat at home to Carlisle, after which Gilchrist was promptly dropped, along with Ian Turner and Bobby Stokes. He was to appear twice more, curiously both times in September at The Valley, where he had started his career. A substitute in the 2-1 League Cup exit, he then made his final appearance in an abject performance in the League, which ended in a 6-2 defeat.

Looking back, Paul says he was always a confidence player and so the Cup win should have been the making of him but, after McMenemy dropped him so readily, he needed to accept that his future lay elsewhere.

Unfortunately, his next move – to Alhafi in Saudi Arabia – was to prove disastrous. Paul's wife, Corinne, didn't want to go, but they considered the offer substantial enough to warrant him signing a year's contract and living there on his own. When he arrived just before Christmas, he found that the promises of a "palace" to live in and many of the other details were entirely without substance.

Much worse, though, was what happened on the pitch. His first match was in the capital, Riyadh, where, punched and spat on by the opposition, he was given little protection by the referee. It was the same in the next game in Jeddah: "it was an absolute nightmare."

Corinne flew out for Christmas but, when it came time to go home, a trip which Paul was planning to make with her, the club had lost his passport. Then he told the Sheikh who owned the club that he was unhappy that so many promises had been broken. It was the Sheikh who had made the promises in the first place, though, and anyone who has worked in the Middle East knows that offering forthright views is a recipe for disaster. A row followed, Paul asked to be released from the contract and duly returned to Southampton.

There was some talk of suing the Saudi team but, in the end, the Alhafi contract was declared void and McMenemy welcomed Paul back, albeit in the

Reserves. There was an offer of a contract at Aldershot but Paul saw the Fourth Division, less than a year after winning the Cup, as too big a step down. Then, in March, Ian St John invited him to join Third Division Portsmouth.

Although he was ever-present for the rest of that 1976-77 season, Paul regrets this move as the biggest mistake of his life. He was booed from first kick to last and to him it seemed that he took the blame for all the club's ills. Having narrowly missed relegation and sacked St John, Pompey finished bottom under Jimmy Dickinson the next season. By then, Paul had played his last League game for the club, surviving just three games longer than Bobby Stokes.

He had one more first-team appearance to come, though, in the League Cup at Swindon in August 1978. He scored in a 4-2 defeat and the Robins promptly put in a bid to buy him. Having decided to join them, he heard that Sheffield Wednesday were interested, but he didn't want to move north. Swindon, a Third Division club on the rise, included Chris Kamara, Bryan Hamilton and Andy Rowland. Paul didn't command a regular place and, in March 1980, moved on to Fourth Division Hereford.

It was a repeat of his arrival at Pompey: ever-present to the end of the season and just survive the drop – in this case requiring re-election to the Football League. He saved his first goal for the final game at Rochdale. It would be his last in competitive football – and, indeed, his last competitive game. Two months later, in a goalless pre-season friendly against Wolves, behind locked doors at their training ground, a less-than-friendly tackle on his standing leg snapped a cruciate ligament. From playing before 100,000 at Wembley, four years before, he had ended his career in a game that nobody saw – although it would take a year of unavailing treatment to confirm that he was, in fact, finished at 30.

It was a triple let-down for Paul. For a start, the offending Wolverhampton player failed to enquire after him: "If you injure someone you always check to see how they are afterwards, but I never heard from anyone at Wolves." Hereford might have softened the blow had they ever honoured an oral promise to pay a signing-on fee; and then, to cap it all, requests to both Southampton and Swindon for a testimonial – of the kind sometimes awarded when a career is cut short by injury – were turned down, "because there were no dates available."

A lesser character would have been quite bitter, but Paul was getting on with Life-after-Football – starting with a venture that became a huge success.

He and a partner opened a fitness centre catering for businesses in Swindon, the first of its type. It was so successful in fact that, after seven years, 12 similar places had opened in competition. Accepting that the best days of the business were past, he closed it down and moved near to Tunbridge Wells. He there took a job with BMW (*right*), where he is an after-sales/service adviser.

His son, Luke, is a Liverpool supporter.

Mick Channon

After showing great loyalty to the club and playing three seasons of Second Division football, during which time he kept his England place, Mick decided it was time to move on and, in the summer of 1977, signed for Manchester City for £300,000.

He found his two seasons at Man City "interesting" but they had their problems. He "struggled" for the first year, but "then Malcolm Allison arrived as manager. After that I played quite well."

In that second, 1978-79, season, Mick played three times against the newly-promoted Saints, losing in both League games and the quarter-final of the League Cup. That was a "very good" Southampton side, he recalls, though many a fan would endorse Ivan Golac's verdict – in *Match of the Millennium* – that all they needed to win that Cup that season was Mick Channon.

Those fans would soon have him back. He fell out with Allison during pre-season training and, in September 1979, re-signed for the Saints.

> I can't say I enjoyed my time at City although I did enjoy Manchester as a place. But the team was in transformation, managers were changing and there was a lot of politics.

To say that he settled back well would be an under-statement: it would be more than two years before he missed a game. He was initially paired up-front with Phil Boyer, the man who had been bought to replace him. They provided the finishing touches to some dazzling approach-play, seldom moreso, perhaps, than in a 4-1 demolition of Nottingham Forest in November 1979 – a performance that underlined, for Golac, what might have been at Wembley eight months earlier.

And then Mick's great friend, Kevin Keegan, arrived to play alongside him for two seasons. This glorious period in the club's history ended for both Channon and Keegan in the summer of 1982. After a four-month period in which Mick played for more clubs than in the previous 16 years – Caroline Hills (Hong Kong), Newcastle and Bristol Rovers – he then joined Norwich City:

Early in his second coming, Channon – here seen wriggling the ball away from Shilton to score the Saints' second goal – had a chance to prove Golac's point in the 4-1 defeat of Forest.

I had a great time. Two-and-a-half years and I only
ever had a monthly contract. I didn't want anything
more in case I had to pack in.

Under the management of Ken Brown and Mel
Machin, the Canaries won the League Cup in 1985.
Mick enjoyed "a good craic in the twilight of my
career" and is quick to credit some good young
players, including Dave Watson, Steve Bruce, Mark
Barham and Peter Mendham: "I was 36 and it was a
great opportunity to go to Wembley and have my son
there" – an under-statement, given that Michael Jr
joined his dad on the pitch and paraded the Cup.

Channon and son show off
Norwich's League Cup.

Next came a call from Alan Ball, who was
manager of Portsmouth. He asked Mick to join him
at Fratton Park and, although the fans "took a little
while to warm to me," he won them over and enjoyed extending his career: "we
just missed out on promotion and it was a good team. The fans were good, but
I've been fortunate: wherever I went, I got on all right with the fans."

At 38 years of age, Mick accepted the inevitable: "I didn't give football up, it
gave me up. I wanted to play on as long as I could, but eventually you become
too old and you have to do something else."

He is glad he kept playing so long, but accepts that he is now paying the
penalty for some bad injuries – not to mention all the injections that enabled him
to play some matches he might prudently have sat out. He nevertheless considers
himself "one of the lucky ones," who has been very fortunate to go on to
something else that he is interested in.

As a footballer, Mick had owned a small farm where he bought and bred
horses. What was always a passion changed from being a hobby to a business. He
believes that, to an extent, he got lucky, buying the right horses and having some

Dressed for the occasion: Ascot 1999.

decent winners; but anyone who knows Mick
knows he makes his own luck through a
combination of hard work and endless
enthusiasm.

He began to learn the intricacies of
training with John Baker in Bampton, North
Devon. He took a few of his own horses and
trained as Baker's assistant, then moved to
work with Ken Cunningham-Brown at
Stockbridge before starting on his own in
Lambourne, little more than two years after
he finished playing.

Finally he settled at West Ilsley. Mick
bought the premises, previously owned by

HM The Queen, from the Privy Purse in 1999. There he trains 150 horses and employs over 60 staff: "I have moved on to have some nice places and train for some very rich people, which makes life that little bit easier."

His ambition now is to win a Classic. He has been close several times but recognises that, in a very competitive business, if he doesn't achieve his goal, he'll get up the next morning and go to work until, hopefully, it does come along: "having a winner and scoring a goal are similar feelings, they give you a high and every time you win you want another winner."

Mick manages at least one family outing each season to the new stadium, where the largest suite bears his name – although his most poignant visit to that neighbourhood of late was to St Mary's Church, for the funeral of Ted Bates.

Invited by Ted's family to make the players' tribute to his first manager, Channon's typically irreverent, yet thoughtfully-crafted, response was an eloquent reminder that the 15 year-old lad who had signed for Bates was now an elder statesman at the club.

Statesman or not, his opinions on football and Southampton FC are as forthright as ever.

The elder statesman delivers his tribute to Ted Bates

> People blame directors or players but the heart of Southampton is in the fans. Directors, managers and players are just caretakers – the club will go on because of the fans who pass it down to their kids and grand kids. I am very proud that my lads are Saints fans just as my Dad passed his love of the club to me.
>
> Fans have the right to say what they want about directors and players because they'll turn up the next week and carry on supporting. We must never forget that a football club belongs to the supporters, to the people, not to any person or persons. And the Saints are a club for the region, spreading into Dorset and Wiltshire, where I am from.

Mick has two children, Michael and Nicola, from his first marriage to Jane and two children, Jack and India, from his second marriage to Jill. He has two grandchildren. His mum, Betty, also lives on campus at West Ilsley.

> The two loves of my life have been football and horses. Horses was my hobby but has become my life and I certainly don't regret anything.

Peter Osgood

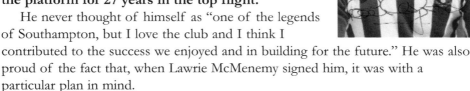

Ossie was to stay with the Saints until the end of 1977. In that time, he played a significant part in an exciting Cup-Winners' Cup run and was a regular for the first third of the promotion season that followed. He has always been proud of the legacy that he and his team-mates left the club, which was the platform for 27 years in the top flight.

He never thought of himself as "one of the legends of Southampton, but I love the club and I think I contributed to the success we enjoyed and in building for the future." He was also proud of the fact that, when Lawrie McMenemy signed him, it was with a particular plan in mind.

> Lawrie was very honest with me. He just said "Ossie, I've got a five-year plan and I'm going to build a side around you." Considering that he had Mick Channon and Terry Paine, I thought that was fantastic.

In reality, the five-year plan finished for Peter within four years, but the statistics don't lie. He played over 150 games, scoring nearly one goal every four matches. When the end came, it was partly for personal reasons: "I was going through a divorce, so it was messy off the field. Lawrie sent me to Norwich on loan for a month. That didn't work and I came back, but I knew I had to get away."

So he joined new NASL franchise, Philadelphia Fury, as their first international signing: "I was probably very selfish but I needed to get my head right. It was a sad time for me, leaving my two kids behind, and I hated it over there. But it was my profession and I had to make a living."

Despite having been a major name in the game for 13 years, he was still only 31 and, by modern standards, would probably still have at least four years at the top. But he lasted only six months in Philadelphia – for one goal in 22 games – and came home for a second spell at Chelsea, where Ken Shellito was the manager. A one-cap England full-back – Terry Paine had made his full-international debut in the same game in Czechoslovakia – Shellito's last season as a Chelsea first-teamer had been Osgood's first.

Their reunion in December 1978 was short-lived: within the month, Shellito was sacked. Osgood would remain to play 10 times in 10 months.

> I should never have gone back there. I should have stayed with the Saints. Before I went out to the States, Lawrie offered me a two-year contract and I should have stuck with it. The players we had then were awesome. Alan Ball, Phil Boyer and Ted MacDougall were top-quality players. I could have played in that side for another three years. I could even have moved back and played sweeper if Lawrie wanted me to. He had played me there a couple of times.

I'd had a great career and enjoyed my time. I had won medals, played in Cup Finals, played for England and been to the World Cup in 1970. I never wanted to drop down the divisions, so I called it a day. I had a year off and moved back with my parents. I enjoyed myself playing golf and going racing.

But he eventually reached "the point where you realise there is not a lot of money left in the bank and you have to go out and earn a living." He was living in Windsor and learned that the *Union Inn*, which "was run by an old chap called Jack Eyers, who knew my dad," was up for sale: "it was a lovely pub in Old Windsor, looking out on the castle, but it was run down and only taking about £250 a week."

The *Union Inn*, as depicted on the Christmas card from Ossie and Hutch

Ossie bought it and invited his old friend and former Chelsea team-mate, Ian Hutchinson, who was working at Stamford Bridge as commercial manager, to come and discuss doing it up and running it together.

We met in a lovely pub called the *Bells of Ousley*, on the river in Windsor. He said "this is fantastic," but I had to put him straight and tell him this wasn't the pub. When he saw the *Union*, he wasn't impressed but I convinced him we could do a lot with it and we did. We built the business up and had it for five years before selling it for a good profit.

Then I got a 'phone call from a guy called Colin Deaton, who had been talking to Alan Ball and wanted me to work for *Butlins* and *Pontins* holiday camps, doing football coaching. It involved a ridiculous amount of travelling – from Barry Island to Tenby in Wales, then Minehead, Perinporth, Plymouth and Bognor. Doing that circuit every week, with only one day off every week, was unbelievably hard but I had to earn a living.

Before long, Alan Ball, who was now manager of Portsmouth, offered him the job of Youth-team coach. Peter immersed himself working with the kids and played a part in developing a good crop of players, including Darren Anderton, Liam Daish, Darryl Powell, Kit Symons and Andy Awford.

> After a heavy defeat at Tottenham, I went in to see Bally and told him I must be doing something wrong. He told me he didn't care about winning Leagues, as long as we were producing players. I'll always remember that because I thought it was a lovely thing to say. And that's what I did, produce players, and we played some lovely football. I enjoyed it.

It all came to an end when chairman Jim Gregory sacked him. It left a sour taste in the mouth and Ossie decided it was time to get out of football. He "didn't know what to do next and it was a bit worrying, but that was where the holiday camp experience paid off. When it rained, I had been expected to do a question-and-answer session, so that experience led me into the after-dinner circuit. I've been all over the world and, apart from the travelling, I really enjoy it."

Peter continued to support Chelsea and Southampton and shared the role of hosting "On The Line" at THE SAINT, with Peter Rodrigues and Hugh Fisher, until his sudden death on 1 March 2006.

He left his widow, Lynn, and their son, Darren. He also had two sons, Anthony and Mark, from his first marriage.

Top: Saints fan, Darren Osgood, dons a Chelsea shirt for a photo with The Special One – and Jose Mourinho, too.
Bottom: Tim Manns and his rotating "On The Line" threesome are joined on the pitch, at half-time during the 2005 quarter-final match against Manchester United, by Paul Gilchrist.
Left to right: Peter Rodrigues, Peter Osgood, Paul Gilchrist, Hugh Fisher, Tim Manns.

Jim McCalliog

Glasgow-born McCalliog spent his entire professional career in England. After joining Leeds United as an amateur, he turned professional at Chelsea, where he had a few games before going on to make a career – winning five Scottish caps along the way – with Sheffield Wednesday, Wolves and Manchester United. Then, in 1975, he joined the Saints, five years after Ted Bates had struck him off his shopping list, not wanting, he told the Board, to "risk his Achilles trouble."

Another of the team to play his last game for the club within 12 months of the Final, he gave way to Alan Ball, who "liked to play" in Jim's central position.

> Lawrie tried playing me on the right but, to be honest, it didn't really work. Young Stevie Williams was coming up as well. What Bally wanted really was two young lads to run around for him because obviously he was losing his legs a little bit then. So he got Steve on his right and Nick Holmes to the left and that meant he could stay central and knock the ball around.

Jim went to Chicago Sting in the summer of 1977 with Bill Foulkes, a sometime United team-mate. A year in the USA was followed by a brief spell as player-coach with Lynn Oslo in Norway. He then received two offers from England: one from Tommy Docherty, who'd managed him both at Chelsea and United, to join him as a squad player at First Division Derby County; the other from Willie Bell, whose Lincoln City were about to become rooted at the foot of Division III.

Given the option of which of these former Scottish internationals to work under, he decided upon Bell. That may seem an odd choice, but Lincoln's up-and-coming young coach, Ian Branfoot, had just gone to join his former boss, Lawrie McMenemy, at Southampton.

So the two-year contract on offer was as player-coach and – further to his Norwegian taster – McCalliog wanted to "find out if I was going to be any good at coaching." Within two months, though, Bell had quit, to be born again as football coach for the Campus Crusade of Christ in America.

Bell's last match in charge proved to be McCalliog's last as a player. He became caretaker-manager for a couple of games, pending Colin Murphy's appointment as manager. Like McMenemy, Murphy had never played in the Football League. Unlike McMenemy, his other credentials did not impress McCalliog: "I told him I didn't want to play for him and asked him to make me an offer to settle my contract. Unfortunately, they told me they couldn't afford to do that." The outcome was that Jim was no longer either a coach or a first-teamer and, before long, he was being suspended for refusing to train.

Eventually, some four months after his last game, a settlement of his contract was negotiated and McCalliog walked away from football completely.

> In a daft kind of way, that was easy. I loved football, and everything about it, but I had got myself a reputation as a bit of a rebel. It was fair to a certain extent, but unfair in other ways. I was never shy to say if I had an opinion or thought something was wrong. I wouldn't go against managers or coaches, but I would say if I thought things wouldn't work or benefit the team. I was outspoken, I suppose, so maybe that made it easier to leave football.
>
> There were a lot of people, Colin Murphy for one, who had come into the game and had never played at any level. They were good at talking, especially to directors, but I always thought the players who had played the game were far better than coaches who didn't really know what was happening on a football field.

Moreover, he felt that the game was generally going through "a bad patch, with not a lot of flair about – and I was a flair player." He "wasn't bitter about coming out of the game, but the one thing I didn't want to do was keep going back to my old clubs and hanging about." In fact, Jim says the group of former team-mates he has spent most time with are those from Southampton.

> That's because of Ossie and the others. They were great lads and we had a fantastic spirit. The hardest thing in my career had been losing the 1966 Cup Final as a Sheffield Wednesday player, having been 2-0 up against Everton. To go back as part of the Saints team, 10 years later, and win was unbelievable.

After leaving the game, Jim put money into his wife's brothers' business but decided he wanted to do something for himself. He admits to having spent a fair amount of time on the customer side of the bar so, when his local landlord suggested going behind the bar, he was quickly attracted to the idea. He took over his first pub in Lytham St Anne's in 1979: "I've only really had two jobs: football and the licence trade – and I've loved them both."

He was tempted back into the game in 1990, as manager of Halifax Town, but life at that level didn't suit him. He settled near York with his second wife in 1995. They ran the *George and Dragon*, on the banks of the River Wharfe at Wetherby, for a while but then Jim, divorced again, took over the *Hare & Hounds* in Riccall, just north of Selby. He left there towards the end of 2005 to take over running a pub in Leeds.

When Harrogate-based fan, Pete Brook, popped in to the *George and Dragon* in Wetherby in 2001 – to get signed a photo of the Wembley 1976 celebrations – he was photographed himself with landlord McCalliog (*left*).

Bobby Stokes

"You're off the list." Those were Lawrie McMenemy's first words, after the final whistle at Wembley, to Bobby Stokes, who had been on the transfer list for most of the season. They made Bobby feel that he was "half-way there", moving on from being "a sort of make-weight at The Dell: the type of player who had to look at the team-sheet every week to make sure he was playing."

Explaining that reaction, in an interview early in the following season, he said he now felt "established and that's a great feeling."

> Before our winning Cup run, I envied players like Mike Channon, and, before him, Terry Paine. They were so outstanding they made their shirts virtually their own property. The only way anyone else was to wear those shirts was if their owners were injured or playing international matches. It was an honour to take over either position for any reason. I truly wanted to be in the same class.

Words of hope and ambition from a player whose stay at The Dell was, sadly, coming to its end: his eighth start of the season in March would be his last for the club – just 15 months after he appeared to have rescued a faltering career.

Having joined as an apprentice in 1966, he accepted that he'd never fully established himself. During his season on the transfer list, he had turned down the chance to join Portsmouth. If that rejection of his home-town club surprised many people, Stokes felt that a "local" transfer was just what he didn't want. If he was going to leave Southampton, he would prefer a "total change of scenery."

Soon after declining that move, his chance to re-establish himself in the first team came along. In a bid to improve a very poor away record, McMenemy decided to change from a 4-3-3 formation to 4-4-2, moving Stokes forward and dropping Osgood a little deeper. It could hardly have worked better. In his first match back in the side, the week before Christmas 1975, Saints won away for the first time that season – 2-0 at The Hawthorns. They would not lose again until the Saturday before the Sixth Round, the end of a 16-match unbeaten run.

This was certainly the golden period in his time with the Saints but, despite the manager's reassuring words at Wembley – perhaps spoken in the excitement of the moment – Bobby might as well have remained on the list.

He played in the 1976-77 opener but, just as for Turner and Gilchrist, the defeat by Carlisle would prove a watershed. The three players were all dropped and, when Ted MacDougall signed a month later, Stokes's fate was sealed. Two months after that eighth and last game of his season, he left, on a free transfer, for a summer with the Washington Diplomats.

In August 1977, he returned to Hampshire and this time he did join Pompey. But all his earlier reservations were to prove founded and, after a brief and unhappy time at Fratton Park, he dropped out of the League. He had two more spells with the Dips and also turned out for Cheltenham Town, Petersfield United, Dartford, Chichester City, Waterlooville and Whitchurch. He even tried his hand at management with Old Simmarians in 1988, but then left the game completely.

He managed the *Manor House* pub in Cosham for three years and also helped his cousin who owned the *Harbour View* café. Then, in May 1995, at the tragically young age of 44, he died of broncho-pneumonia.

His place in the history of Southampton FC and the hearts of the fans is, of course, assured: indeed, the fans voted for a lounge in the new stadium to be named after him (*right*). But his loss has been felt most keenly by former team-mates.

Peter Osgood, with whom he roomed for four years, would always get "choked up talking about him."

> He was one of my best mates and the funniest lad you ever met in your life. Great to be with. Great company. Just an honest boy. Bobby was the jewel in the dressing room, always larking about and taking the micky. It was great that the goal went to him rather than Mick, Jim or me, who might have been expected to score.

Peter remembered how he learned of Bobby's death. He had rung him on the Saturday, when "his Mum said he wasn't well. Apparently, he played golf on the Sunday but only managed to hit the ball six times and couldn't even hit the ladies' tee [30 yards away] – so he was obviously very ill." Come the Tuesday, Peter was at the Meon Valley Golf Club with Lynn, his wife, when he was summoned, over the tannoy, by Terry Hussey, the general manager: "I said to Lynn, 'This is Bobby'; and Terry told me he had died. I was devastated."

Mick Channon, who had known Bobby longer than anyone at the club, had always found him "a smashing lad… the boy next door who just wanted to play football" and feels that he seemingly "found it hard to adapt to life without football. It was so sad." And David Peach puts an interesting perspective on Bobby's moment of glory.

> I always thought him scoring played a part in his early death. Somebody like Mick, Ossie or Jim would have handled what came next. They had seen it all before, but Bobby was a simple-living lad and he couldn't say "no". He was a lovely fellow and everybody wanted to know him and take him here and there. When all that dried up and he left Southampton, he struggled at Pompey and then he was left alone.

It is clear, then, that Bobby Stokes was a down-to-earth, honest, decent man who wrote his own epitaph on 1 May 1976. In that interview a few months later, he put it very simply.

> Winning the FA Cup was the greatest moment of my life.

Hugh Fisher

Just like Jim McCalliog, Hughie was born in
Glasgow but spent his football career in England.
He had been at Blackpool, where he had shared digs
with Alan Ball and Emlyn Hughes. Having played a
scoring role in the Seasiders' 5-1 win at The Dell at
the end of 1966, he traded one relegation-battling
club for another. It proved the right decision as
Blackpool dropped from the top flight, whereas
Fisher's combination of skill and determination
made a significant contribution to the Saints' survival.

Hugh started the 1976 pre-season still carrying the pelvic injury that had kept
him out of the semi-final and Final. Yet, with Gilchrist no longer in contention
for his place, he hardly missed a game until late November. But then, as his old
digs-mate, Ball, arrived to play alongside the young contender, Steve Williams,
Fisher became a regular in the Reserves – until March 1977.

That month began with Hugh playing for the Reserves, along with four of the
Wembley winners – Turner, Rodrigues, Stokes and McCalliog – in a 2-1 win at
Ipswich. But two weeks later – 10 years and a day after his Saints debut at
Everton – he was starting out for Southport at Darlington. Those 10 years of
service meant that he had been considered for a testimonial. Always the most
modest, self-effacing of men, Hugh wondered whether there would be sufficient
support – it was "probably a confidence thing: I wasn't sure how the public
would view it" – which seems remarkable, given the obvious affection and respect
with which he is remembered.

If Jimmy Melia had had his way, Fisher would never have completed those 10
years at The Dell – or even have been part of Saints' Cup run. While briefly
managing Southport in the summer of 1975, Melia had hoped to tempt his
former Southampton team-mate back to the Lancashire Coast. Hughie never
learned of that interest. But when Southport now came enquiring again – would
he fancy player-management in the Fourth Division? – he got the message.

> The money was good so I talked it through with my wife. Like most players, I had
> to decide what to do next, whether to move into the real world and start my
> education all over again. With the chance to stay in football comes that dream that
> you will end up behind the desk running Arsenal.

But he still had plenty to do on the pitch, playing in Southport's remaining 15
games of that 1976-77 season and missing only one of the next season's 46. Add
in six Cup matches and that's 66 games in a season and two months. Not bad,
considering he was 34 by the end of it – even if he did try to save his legs for a
while by playing himself as sweeper. However he deployed himself, though, he
lacked the resources to keep Southport in the Football League.

The standard was much lower than I was used to. There were some good lads but they weren't as fit as they might have been. They were paid very poor money and there was no cash available to buy players. A couple of times, the wages didn't get paid and the gates were averaging about 2,000.

In fact, they dropped to three figures for the last few home games of that season, when Southport finished one off the bottom. The club was so hard-up that the Board threatened not to seek re-election. But kept afloat by the sale of George Dewsnip to Fort Lauderdale – a $20,000 profit on a discovery of Alan Ball, Sr, who'd arrived free from Preston – and falsely encouraged by the promise of an anonymous loan that never materialised, they went to the vote and survived – only to come 23rd again in 1977-78. This time, they were voted out, Wigan Athletic being elected in their stead.

So Southport were out of the League and Hughie was out of a job. Although he had moved the family to Southport, they had kept their house in Hampshire and so were able to return. Hugh carried on playing at semi-professional level, first with Basingstoke Town and later at Waterlooville. He enjoyed playing with "a great bunch at Waterlooville and was really impressed with their commitment, given that they all had full-time jobs." But, with his knees now becoming very sore after games, he retired from football in 1980.

By this time, he was working for *Schweppes* in sales. Soon after that, he joined *Watneys*, covering the Southampton and Eastleigh area. The company are now *Newcastle Courage* and he is looking forward to retirement and spending more time on the golf course

Always ready to reminisce and with an almost permanent smile, Hugh has no regrets about his playing career. He even managed a wry smile at the memory of contract negotiations at The Dell.

On behalf of *Courage*, the sponsors of the *Echo* Saints Player of the Month award, Hugh Fisher presents Francis Benali with the trophy for September 1998.

I remember one season [1970-71] I had played 42 League matches but, when I went in to see Ted Bates, he managed to convince me I had only had a so-so kind of season and I went away thanking him for not giving me much of an increase. Lawrie was much the same but I respected both of them. Of course, like most players, I didn't know much about the ins-and-outs of running a football club.

One of Hugh's sons, Stuart, played for Bashley and had a trial for the Saints. Stuart and his brother Peter both work in television. Hugh lives in Bishops Waltham with his wife, Claudia.

Paul Bennett

The summer of 1976 was a bittersweet time for Paul. He realised that Lawrie McMenemy had decided it was time for him to move on.

The seeds of discontent had been sown over the annual pay-and-contract review. After playing in almost half the previous season's League matches and having been involved in the Cup run, he was disappointed to be offered only a £6-a-week rise. Paul thought he "was worth more, but Lawrie said he was following government policy." That year's pay-rise limit was, indeed, £6 but, unlike some other years of incomes policy, the restriction for 1975-76 was voluntary and Paul "knew others weren't being told that. So that was it and I went to Reading."

Although he didn't want to go, Bennett realised he had no choice. Initially, when told he was going to Reading, he refused but was told he had no say. The club were getting ready for the Charity Shield and Mel Blyth was an injury-doubt, so Paul was expecting to play. When he was told to talk to Reading again, he said he wanted to wait until after Saturday.

> I was told I wouldn't be involved, even on the bench. Then I decided there was no reason to stay. It is interesting to compare how things are now with my time. Alec Perkins at Weston Park School and Denis Huxtable at Itchen Grammar School were responsible for bringing young players to the club. Then Mike Smith, who chose me for my first representative game at under-14 level, and Bill Ellerington, when I joined Saints, all made it clear that you were joining a club that would give you a chance to come through and get to the first team. As a young footballer, you wanted to play for your home club, not Chelsea or Arsenal – I had the chance to join Spurs but preferred to sign for Saints – so it was a wrench to leave.

His first season at Reading brought an early Cup exit at Hereford – where Terry Paine, released too soon by McMenemy in Paul's opinion, was man-of-the-match – and then, much worse, relegation to the Fourth Division. Following such a season, he "didn't expect much" from the contract review to which he was entitled. He was nevertheless disappointed to be told "they had already reviewed it and I wasn't getting any more."

But demotion meant a change of manager. Paine was a red-hot favourite for the job, but Maurice Evans was promoted from within and persuaded a disaffected Bennett to make a fresh start. He finished the next, 1977-78, season strongly and missed only one game in 1978-79 when Reading interrupted Southampton's progress to the League Cup Final, by taking them to a replay, and won their division.

A settled "back-five" had missed only two League games between them and set a club record for clean sheets: 26 in the season, including the entire 11-match run-in. All of which should perhaps have laid the foundation for a longer stay but, when the expected pay rise was not forthcoming, Paul moved to Aldershot for a further three seasons in Division Four, before dropping out of League football. He continued to play, for Peter Price at Road Sea Southampton, while starting a full-time career in community work.

> I loved working with Pricey because he is so honest and he did what he said he would do. He expected the same and he couldn't understand the pro game. He felt there were people saying things they wouldn't do. We established Road Sea as a very good Southern League side but, when Peter decided to come out of it, I left and played for a couple of local sides to keep fit.

For four years he worked on the sport-and-community side at Oaklands School in Lordshill but, unable to advance because he wasn't a teacher, he moved on to 86 East Point Community Centre, Thornhill, where he is Group Director.

Despite the long hours this job demands, Paul found time in 1998 to organise a massive celebration of Ted Bates's first 60 seasons with the Saints, to coincide with the launch of Ted's biography, *Dell Diamond*. His fantasy that this could be a modestly-priced event – "for people like my mum" – was realised when the sponsorship he solicited enabled him to bring from overseas the likes of Terry Paine, John Sydenham, Ron Davies and Tony Knapp to mingle with the fans at two sell-out sittings, lasting over 12 hours.

When he reflects on the Cup-winning squad, he is quick to point out that, although he was near-neighbours and friends with Paul Gilchrist and David Peach, the whole squad were friends: "I roomed with Peter Rodrigues, or sometimes Jim Steele, and got on well with both. The team ethic meant we all wanted to do well for each other and to be in the team. I would have played left wing if asked."

He also admits to having got on reasonably well with Saints' nearest rivals: "I was friendly with Ray Hiron at Pompey and we played together at Reading and then I used to see him when he was at the Mountbatten Sports Centre."

Paul looks back on his footballing career as "quite a challenge" but is happy that he did what he "wanted to do."

> I saw the heights and the depths; and the depths were low. Sadly, because they could only play 11 players, I was often on the sidelines. I find it interesting now that you have players who are happy to sit on the sidelines and collect a wage. I just wanted to play. But the heights were great: I played against some of the best players ever in this country and I think I came out even; but then I would say that.

Paul's partner of 20 years is Annette. His son Alistair is from his prior marriage.

Pat Earles

A modest man, Pat nevertheless knew his worth: "I like to think whenever I played I made a contribution and that I had a reasonable goals-to-games ratio."

Yet if it was hard enough for him, in the opening games of the 1976-77 season, to get a couple of starts as the understudy to Osgood or Channon, it was even worse when Ted MacDougall arrived in September to command a place for the rest of the season. Pat would get but one more start so a move to Reading, in January, gave him the opportunity to establish himself as a first-team player. He was offered a loan move but George Horsfall advised him to take a permanent transfer if possible. He admits he was just glad to get first-team football.

In his six-and-a-half seasons at Reading, he was top-scorer in each of his first three full seasons and finished with 85 goals, making him No.10 in the Royals' all-time scoring list – all of which he finds "pretty satisfying, but you always want to make it with your home-town club."

He tended to score especially freely in the League Cup but drew a blank, in 1978-79, when the Royals took the Wembley-bound Saints to a replay. He reckons Terry Gennoe saved the Saints in a goalless draw at Elm Park that Reading should have won in front of their season's best crowd, by far, of 24,000: "Gennoe made one particular save from Lawrie Sanchez that was outstanding. I also had one chance, where I claim I hit the volley too well." He found it strange to come back and play at The Dell in the replay.

> The atmosphere was great but it was very odd to be on the other side when they started singing, *Oh! When the Saints…* The crowd at The Dell always created an amazing atmosphere.

Pat retired at 28 with long-term lower back, and hamstring, problems that affected his pace and mobility, a key part of his game. Reading manager Maurice Evans gave him a free transfer so, as he puts it, he decided to take control of his life rather than wait to see what might happen. He joined the probation service to work with young offenders, though not as a probation officer. He later went to university in Southampton in order to qualify. Meanwhile, he played for Road Sea.

I knew I could cope with the injuries at that level. I enjoyed my football most in those five years at that level. I was making a living, anyway, so there was nowhere near the pressure. Of course, Paul Bennett was there and maybe sometimes people wanted to make a point, because Road Sea were a bit unpopular, and also because we were ex-pros –but it was never an issue for me. We wanted to maintain high standards and we had quality players.

When Reading entertained the Saints in the League Cup, the cover of the special matchday programme featured Bennett (*left*) and Earles.

Earles recalls manager Peter Price demanding success, an attitude borne out by a sign that hung in the dressing room: *First is first and second is nowhere.* "That summed Peter up. We got promotion from the Southern Premier League in my first season, which was a relief because that was what I was signed to do." He now has that sign as a souvenir.

Having done quite a lot of coaching with kids, Pat decided he wanted to work with youngsters in an environment where he might help to bring about change. Having found football to be quite a selfish profession, he liked the idea of using his time to make a contribution in something valuable: "I found doing the degree to be hard graft but my football was a great release from that. Something I could do without thinking too much."

Pat was never a good watcher of football and, since finishing in the pro' game, hasn't watched at all. He played for ex-Saints for a number of years but rarely mentions, these days, that he used to play football. Whenever he does, though, he finds that people are always interested. He was working in Winchester prison when Saints got to the Cup Final in 2003 and was amazed at how a *Sun* newspaper article, looking back at Saints' previous Final, got round and created a lot of interest among inmates and prison officers. He believes having been in football can create a bridge to form relationships and friendships.

Looking back, I don't think you realise how lucky you are at the time to be playing football for a living: it is only when you get older and look back and reflect. I remember sitting in The Dell's away-team dressing-room when the apprentices were told if they were being retained. I was lucky to never have been let go but I saw how it affected those who were.

Pat lives in the Fareham area – not far from where he grew up – with his wife, Sandra. They have two sons, Ian and Tom.

Gerry O'Brien

Gerry started the 1975-76 season with a seven-game run in the first team, but lost his place to his good friend, Hugh Fisher. His only involvement for the rest of the season was as a substitute. Having come on in both the Fourth and Fifth Rounds, he remained on the bench during the quarter-final at Bradford. Then, as the transfer deadline loomed the following week, he was offered a move to Swindon Town.

He had been at The Dell six years without fulfilling expectations: Ted Bates had told the Board that, once the part-timer from Clydebank was training full-time, "he could become a younger edition of Paine." That demonstrably hadn't happened and he was now 26. So, although he didn't really want to go – and readily admits he wasn't forced out – he accepted what he describes as a good offer from manager Danny Williams.

> In hindsight, I wish I hadn't moved because I would like to have been involved in the last two rounds of the Cup. It was disappointing not to be there when they won, but that is just one of those things.

Gerry stayed at home to watch the Final and was very happy for all his old team-mates: "I had a great time with the club, got married in Southampton and my two sons were born in the city."

He remained at Swindon for the rest of that season and the whole of the next, but missed a lot of games with a cartilage injury. Given a free transfer in 1977, he returned to Clydebank. He moved on to Hibernian after a season, potentially to form a right-wing partnership with Ally MacLeod, who'd played a few times for the Saints in 1973-74. But while MacLeod was ever-present in 1978-79, O'Brien managed only two starts.

So it was back to bricklaying, his trade while playing part-time for Clydebank. He started his own building company which his sons, Stephen and Paul, now work in. After a hip replacement, he is a regular golfer.

In the years that followed his football career, he kept in touch with fellow-Scots, Fisher and Steele, and is still good friends with MacLeod. Gerry lives in Clydebank with his wife, Maureen.

Player Records

Compiled by Gary Chalk

APPEARANCES and GOALS in LEAGUE and CUP games, during each player's career with ENGLISH & SCOTTISH LEAGUE CLUBS.

The records for Steele and O'Brien refer to the competitions in the relevant country

IAN TURNER

6' 0"   12st 5lbs   b. Middlesbrough 17/1/53

CLUBS	SIGNED	LEAGUE		FA CUP		LGE CUP	
		App	*Gls*	*App*	*Gls*	*App*	*Gls*
Huddersfield Town	Oct 70	0	0	0	0	0	0
Grimsby Town *	Feb 72 loan	26	0	1	0	1	0
Walsall	Feb 73 loan	3	0	0	0	0	0
Southampton	Mar 74	77	0	12	0	6	0
Newport County	Mar 78 loan	7	0	0	0	0	0
Lincoln City	Oct 78 loan	7	0	0	0	0	0
Walsall	Jan 79	39	0	0	0	4	0
Luton Town	Feb 80 loan	0	0	0	0	0	0
Halifax Town	Jan 81 loan	5	0	0	0	0	0

* Permanent transfer Mar 72

PETER JOSEPH RODRIGUES

5' 9"   11st 11lbs   b. Canton, Cardiff 21/1/44

CLUBS	SIGNED	LEAGUE		FA CUP		LGE CUP	
		App	*Gls*	*App*	*Gls*	*App*	*Gls*
Cardiff City	May 61	85	2	2	0	8	0
Leicester City	Dec 65	139(1)	6	18(1)	0	11(1)	0
Sheffield Wednesday	Oct 70	162	2	7	0	5	0
Southampton	Jul 75	59	3	8	0	3	0

MELVIN BERNARD BLYTH

6' 1"   11st 11lbs   b. Norwich 28/7/44

CLUBS	SIGNED	LEAGUE		FA CUP		LGE CUP	
		App	*Gls*	*App*	*Gls*	*App*	*Gls*
Scunthorpe United	Nov 67	27	3	0	0	0	0
Crystal Palace	Jul 68	213(3)	9	12	1	19	2
Southampton	Sep 74	104(1)	6	15	0	2	0
Crystal Palace	Nov 77 loan	6	0	0	0	0	0
Millwall	Nov 78	75	0	6	0	4	0

JAMES STEELE

6' 1"   12st 2lbs   b. Edinburgh 11/3/50

CLUBS	SIGNED	LEAGUE		FA CUP		LGE CUP	
		App	Gls	App	Gls	App	Gls
Dundee	Apr 67	74(1)	5	3	0	8	0
Southampton	Jan 72	160(1)	2	16	0	12	0
Rangers	Nov 76 loan	5	0	0	0	0	0

DAVID SIDNEY PEACH

5' 9"   10st 3lbs   b. Bedford 21/1/51

CLUBS	SIGNED	LEAGUE		FA CUP		LGE CUP	
		App	Gls	App	Gls	App	Gls
Gillingham	Sep 69	186(1)	30	9	0	9	1
Southampton	Jan 74	221(3)	34	21	6	20	2
Swindon Town	Mar 80	52(1)	2	3	0	4	0
Orient	Mar 82	47	6	2	0	1	0

PAUL ANTHONY GILCHRIST

5' 11"   12st 4lbs   b. Dartford 5/1/51

CLUBS	SIGNED	LEAGUE		FA CUP		LGE CUP	
		App	Gls	App	Gls	App	Gls
Charlton Athletic	Mar 68	5(2)	0	0	0	0	0
Luton Town	loan	0	0	0	0	0	0
Cambridge United	Jan 70 loan	0	0	0	0	0	0
Fulham	Mar 71 loan	0	0	0	0	0	0
Doncaster Rovers	Jul 71	22	8	1	0	0	0
Southampton	Mar 72	96(11)	17	10	2	6(1)	1
Portsmouth	Mar 77	38(1)	3	0	0	2	0
Swindon Town	Aug 78	10(7)	6	4	2	1	0
Hereford United	Mar 80	11	1	0	0	0	0

JAMES McCALLIOG

5' 9"   10st 5lbs   b. Glasgow 23/9/46

CLUBS	SIGNED	LEAGUE		FA CUP		LGE CUP	
		App	Gls	App	Gls	App	Gls
Chelsea	Sep 63	7	2	0	0	5	1
Sheffield Wednesday	Oct 65	150	19	18	5	6	3
Wolverhampton Wanderers	Aug 69	158(5)	34	9	4	9(1)	4
Manchester United	Mar 74	31	7	1	0	5(1)	0
Southampton	Feb 75	70(2)	8	10	3	2	0
Lincoln City (player/coach)	Sep 78	9	0	0	0	0	0

NICHOLAS CHARLES HOLMES

5' 11"   11st 11lbs   b. Woolston, Southampton 11/11/54

CLUBS	SIGNED	LEAGUE		FA CUP		LGE CUP	
		App	Gls	App	Gls	App	Gls
Southampton	Nov 72	437(7)	56	45	2	38	6

MICHAEL ROGER CHANNON

6' 0"   12st 11lbs   b. Orcheston 28/11/48

CLUBS	SIGNED	LEAGUE		FA CUP		LGE CUP	
		App	Gls	App	Gls	App	Gls
Southampton	Dec 65	388(3)	157	34(2)	17	24	11
Manchester City	Jul 77	71(1)	24	3(1)	0	11(1)	4
Southampton	Sep 79	119	28	6	1	4	0
Newcastle United	Aug 82	4	1	0	0	0	0
Bristol Rovers	Oct 82	4(5)	0	0	0	0(1)	0
Norwich City	Dec 82	84(4)	16	10	2	14	7
Portsmouth	Aug 85	34	6	2	0	4	0

PETER LESLIE OSGOOD

6' 1"   12st 6lbs   b. Windsor 20/2/47 d. 1/3/06

CLUBS	SIGNED	LEAGUE		FA CUP		LGE CUP	
		App	Gls	App	Gls	App	Gls
Chelsea	Sep 64	276(3)	103	33	19	30	10
Southampton	Mar 74	122(4)	28	12	1	9	2
Norwich City	Nov 76 loan	3	0	0	0	0	0
Chelsea	Dec 78	9	2	1	0	0	0

ROBERT WILLIAM THOMAS STOKES

5' 7"   10st 2lbs   b. Portsmouth 30/1/51 d. 30/5/95

CLUBS	SIGNED	LEAGUE		FA CUP		LGE CUP	
		App	Gls	App	Gls	App	Gls
Southampton	Feb 68	194(22)	40	17	7	11(1)	5
Portsmouth	Aug 77	23(1)	2	2	1	3	0

HUGH DONNELLY FISHER

5' 8"   10st 8lbs   b. Glasgow 9/1/44

CLUBS	SIGNED	LEAGUE		FA CUP		LGE CUP	
		App	Gls	App	Gls	App	Gls
Blackpool	Aug 62	52(3)	1	3	0	7(1)	0
Southampton	Mar 67	297(5)	7	22(2)	3	17(1)	1
Southport (player/manager)	Mar 77	60	0	2	0	4	0

PAUL REGINALD BENNETT

6' 0"   12st 6lbs   b. Southampton 4/2/52

CLUBS	SIGNED	LEAGUE		FA CUP		LGE CUP	
		App	*Gls*	*App*	*Gls*	*App*	*Gls*
Southampton	Nov 69	116	1	7	1	8	0
Reading	Jul 76	105	3	7	0	11	0
Aldershot	Aug 79	112(1)	2	6	0	6	0

PATRICK JOHN EARLES

5' 7"   10st 0lbs   b. Titchfield 22/3/55

CLUBS	SIGNED	LEAGUE		FA CUP		LGE CUP	
		App	*Gls*	*App*	*Gls*	*App*	*Gls*
Southampton	Nov 72	4(8)	1	0(1)	0	1	1
Reading	Jan 77	240(7)	68	9	6	22	11

GERALD O'BRIEN

5' 6"   9st 9lbs   b. Glasgow 10/11/49

CLUBS	SIGNED	LEAGUE		FA CUP		LGE CUP	
		App	*Gls*	*App*	*Gls*	*App*	*Gls*
Clydebank	May 68	46(5)	7	2	0	2	1
Southampton	Mar 70	66(12)	2	6(4)	0	2(1)	0
Bristol Rovers	Mar 74 loan	3	0	0	0	0	0
Swindon Town	Mar 76	24(3)	0	0	0	2	0
Clydebank	Aug 77	24	1	1	0	3	0
Hibernian	May 78	2(5)	0	0	0	1	0

Sources

All Hagiology titles owe a debt of gratitude to the researches, collections and collations of Duncan Holley and Gary Chalk:

Saints: a Complete Record of Southampton Football Club, 1885-1987, Breedon, 1987.
The Alphabet of the Saints: a complete who's who of Southampton FC, ACL & Polar, 1992.
In That Number: a post-war chronicle of Southampton FC, Hagiology Publishing, 2003.

The other reference books on which we have constantly drawn have been the relevant seasons of those dependable annuals – the *News of the World Football Annual* and the *Rothmans Football Yearbook* (reconstituted as the *Sky Sports Football Yearbook* from 2003-04) – and four other invaluable sources:

Mike Collett, *The Guinness Record of the FA Cup*, Guinness Publishing, 1993 (republished as *The Complete Record of the FA Cup*, Sportsbooks, 2003).
Barry J. Hugman (ed.), *The PFA Premier & Football League Players' Records 1946-2005*, Queen Anne Press, 2005.
Jack Rollin, *Rothmans Book of Football Records*, Headline, 1998
Dennis Turner & Alex White (eds.), *The Breedon Book of Football Managers*, 1993

We have also drawn, sometimes with a specific reference in the text, upon the following books and articles:

David Bull, *Dell Diamond: Ted Bates's first 60 seasons with The Saints*, Hagiology Publishing, 1998 (pbk edn, 2004).
David Bull & Bob Brunskell (eds), *Match of the Millennium: The Saints' 100 Most Memorable Matches*, Hagiology Publishing, 2000.
Mike Channon, *Home and Away: an autobiography*, Stanley Paul, 1977.
Archie Gemmill, *Both Sides of the Border: my autobiography*, Hodder & Stoughton, 2005.
Lou Macari, *United – we shall not be moved*, Souvenir Press, 1976.
Chris Newman, interview with Peter Rodrigues, *The Ugly Inside* (souvenir edn), 1996.
Ron Parrott, *Hereford United: the League era*, Desert Island Books, 1998.
Peter Raath, *Soccer Through The Years 1862-2002*, www.soccerthroughtheyears.com, 2002.
Bobby Stokes, "Secrets behind a Fantastic Cup Triumph", *Topical Times Football Book 1977*, D.C.Thompson, 1976.
Geoff Wilde and Michael Braham, *The Sandgrounders: the complete League history of Southport FC*, Palatine Books, 1995.

We have drawn upon two TV programmes:

Match of the Day, BBC 1, 1 May 1976 (excerpts available in the video, *Match of the Day: Southampton FC*, BBC Enterprises, 1991).
Gerry Daly, *Brian Moore Interviews*, BskyB, 1999.

Presentations & Subscriptions

We are pleased to present copies of this book to

Gary Chalk and Duncan Holley, Hagiology Publishing's ever-dependable
providers of statistics, photos and so much else.
Norman Gannaway and Dave Juson, of Hagiology Publishing.
Our associates, in the production of this and other books, at
Southampton FC and the *Southern Daily Echo*.
Tommy Docherty, for his foreword, and each of our interviewees.
Jim Dolbear, Steve Eckersley, Nigel Hale, Andy Kershaw, Ray Mursell,
Chris Newman, George Tomkins and Dave Webster, whose supply
– in some permutation – of memories, photos and scrapbooks
was especially extensive.

1	Ann Chalk, Eastleigh.	30	Dominic Stevens, Woolston.
2	A.M.Quigley, Wimborne.	31	Brian Stevens, Bassett Green.
3	Nigel Burgess, Hoddesdon.	32	John Lovelock, Southampton.
4	Mark Fickling, Rownhams.	33	David Brindley, Gosport.
5	Christine Webster, Sholing.	34	Mark Wood, Newbury.
6	Alan Gosling, Woking.	35	Graham Scott, Southampton.
7	Richard Atkinson, Macclesfield.	36	Therese Scott, Southampton.
8	Mike Lawson, Littlehampton.	37	Karen Arkell, Southampton.
9	Terence S Bruty, Whitchurch.	38	Brian Dawkins, Romsey.
10	Louise Vallis, Bartley.	39	Joan Rosenberg-Summers, Romsey.
11	John Vallis, Bartley.	40	Phil Rawlings, Fair Oak.
12	David Howard, Hartington.	41	Mike Sadler, Chandler's Ford.
13	M.R. Benge, Castellon, Spain.	42	Martyn Wartski, Poole.
14	Lee Curtis, Bournemouth.	43	Ross Taylor, Andover.
15	David Weaver, Warsash.	44	Julian Sutton, Nunhead.
16	Glen Williams, Locks Heath.	45	Hayden Hopkins, Andover.
17	Mike Baker, Hythe.	46	Eric & Craig Holland, Highfield, IoW.
18	John Warren, London.	47	Sean & Callum Kershaw, Chandler's Ford.
19	Paul Dyke, Bournemouth.	48	Michael & Nicholas Weston, Fritham
20	Ted Tarbart, Shanklin, IoW.	49	Janet Formby, NS42L1088.
21	Stephen Cheffy, Crawley.	50	Cliff Hibberd, WSCP9.
22	Andrew Stead, Basingstoke.	51	Ann & Den Macklin, Sholing.
23	Ivor Stead, Basingstoke.	52	Ian Williams, Sholing.
24	David Cheffy, Hedge End.	53	Charlie Hedges, Chandler's Ford.
25	Des Earl, Southampton.	54	Elaine Bushrod, Chandler's Ford.
26	Phil Russell, Warrington.	55	The Ruthen Family, Netley Abbey.
27	Marc Russell, Warrington.	56	Tim Scott, Stourbridge.
28	Toby Manns, Sanderstead.	57	Bob Warren, Chandler's Ford.
29	Roy D. Stevens, Woolston.	58	Leon Simon, Bournemouth.

59 Kate & Peter Horne MBE, Hythe.
60 Paul Streeter, Basingstoke.
61 Geraldine Garrett, Eastleigh.
62 John Hibberd, Southampton.
63 Nick Hiscott, Shirley.
64 Colin Evans, Bognor.
65 Norman Creese, Meonstoke.
66 Geoff Parnham, Amport.
67 Martyn Parnham, Waltham Chase.
68 John Caddy, Upper Shirley.
69 Alan Caddy, Chandler's Ford.
70 Robin Caddy, Upper Shirley.
71 Ross White, Freemantle.
72 Chris Manns, London.

73 Phil Manns, London.
74 Rob Manns, London.
75 Jane Manns, London.
76 Rachel Manns, London.
77 Jamie Manns, London.
78 Sarah Manns, London.
79 Trudy Hayter, Ferndown.
80 Derek Hayter, Sixpenny Handley.
81 James Smith, Chandler's Ford.
82 Javi Igeno, Jerez de la Frontera.
83 John Gill, Fallbrook, California.
84 Roy Willis, Romsey.
85 Brian Smith, Birmingham
86 Andrew House, Chichester

When we were assembling the fans' memories of the Cup Final and trying to convey different kinds of involvement, our several categories included those who followed the game, on TV or radio, from overseas, and those who dressed up for the day, even though they were staying in Southampton. Somehow, there wasn't a group who dressed up to watch TV in a far corner of Hampshire.

Which is why there was no room, in that section, for this recent photo of Steve Mullins with the scarf he wore, as an 11 year-old, at home near Aldershot, "glued to the telly, virtually the whole of the day" – in the way that Nick Holmes has recalled his childhood experience. Steve's nan had created this interest by bring him back a Saints mug from holiday – he has "no idea where they had been" – and then knitting him a scarf and bobble hat to go with it. He wore both to watch the TV but only the scarf has survived: "the hat got nicked at a game at Reading a few years later."

It seemed a pity to waste this space, at the end of the book, when we could be dedicating it to Steve and all those young fans of 1976 – the likes of Andy Kershaw (see pages 67 and 110 above) and fellow nine year-old Paul Dyke – who participated in the Final in front of the TV, a rite of passage on their way to being the live fans of today.

Hagiology Publishing

**"Of all the single-club football histories,
those from the roseate crew
at Southampton are always the ones to relish."**

That is how leading sportswriter, Frank Keating, has described the histories of
Southampton FC that have been produced, since 1998, by Hagiology Publishing.

The five books already published are:

DELL DIAMOND – the story of Ted Bates's first 60 seasons with the Saints.
Initially published as a 366-page hardback in 1998 at £18.99, it was republished,
as a commemorative, paperback edition (£9.99) in 2004, with a special, new
chapter honouring Ted's last six seasons.

MATCH of the MILLENNIUM – accounts of the Saints' 100 most
memorable matches, a 222-page paperback published in 2000 at £12.99.

FULL-TIME at THE DELL – a 240-page paperback published in 2001
at £16.95, this homage to Saints' 103 seasons at The Dell was included in
Frank Keating's *Guardian* selection of "Top Six" sports books of 2001.

IN THAT NUMBER – this 640-page hardback, published in 2003 in full-
colour at £35, is a post-war chronicle of the Saints, with reports on over 2,500
games and profiles of almost 400 players. Said by *BBC Sport OnLine* to "transport
the mere club history to a new dimension" and to "set the yardstick by which
every other club history will now be judged."

SAINTS v POMPEY – this 288-page paperback, published in 2004 at £18.99,
reports on the first 209 games played between these neighbours, from 1899 to
2004, and not only charts the men who have played for both but hears from fans
who have followed both.

**To order any of the above titles direct – with 20% OFF the hardback price
and at least 25% OFF the paperback prices – please contact us
at one of the addresses/numbers opposite.**

Postage extra – but not if we can arrange a pick-up, at St Mary's or elsewhere

---

Formed in 1998, Hagiology Publishing is a collective of four Saints fans committed to the collection and dissemination of accurate information on the history of Southampton FC.

The collective, as photographed at St Mary's during the 2005-06 season.
Left to right: David Bull, Dave Juson, Gary Chalk, Duncan Holley.

This latest venture is Hagiology Publishing's sixth publication – and the fifth within an agreement with Southampton FC and the *Southern Daily Echo* regularly to produce books on aspects of Saints' history.

Details of its five previous publications appear opposite.

The next book in the pipe-line is:

CONSTANT PAINE – a biography of Terry Paine (Autumn 2006)

We welcome enquiries about **TIE A YELLOW RIBBON**. Please contact the appropriate member of the Hagiology collective as indicated below:

Individual (including mail-order) enquiries:
Gary Chalk
47 Doncaster Road
Eastleigh, Hants SO50 5QP
Tel: 032(80) 328435
garyeastleigh@aol.com

All retail and review enquiries:
David Bull
170 Westbury Road
Bristol BS9 3AH
Tel: 0117 962 2042
bull.hagiology@blueyonder.co.uk

Or please visit www.hagiologists.com